The Book of Picture Frames

Claus Grimm

with a supplement by George Szabo

ABARIS BOOKS • NEW YORK

The American edition has been expanded and its layout is new.

Translation by: Nancy M. Gordon and Walter L. Strauss
Responsible Editor: Sebastian Buffa
Designer: Ken Meads

ISBN 0-913870-92-7
Copyright © 1978 by Verlag Georg D.W. Callwey, Munich (German edition)
Copyright © 1981 by Abaris Books, Inc., New York (English translation)
24 West 40th Street, New York, New York 10018
Printed in the United States of America

Contents

Acknowledgements

This book could not have been written without the help and support of the small circle of experts and enthusiasts in the field of picture frames.

My attention was first directed to picture frames by Mr. Leo Cremer of Munich. My thanks go to him for the basic references which led to the collection of materials for this book. The exposition of Italian frames in the Pinakothek Museum in Munich, which he initiated, laid the groundwork for this survey. Just as significant for me were the observations on craftsmanship, on the history and cultural background of frames, which Mr. Paul Levi of London provided. I am deeply indebted to Mr. Matthias Hornsteiner of Munich for his unfailing readiness to supply information on material, technique and production. All three of these also deserve my thanks for the moral support which they provided me in this undertaking.

I have also presumed upon the patience of several enthusiasts for the picture frame as a field of art, particularly Mr. Jan Lowe of Oxford and Dr. P.P.J. van Thiel of Amsterdam. Valuable suggestions were also given by Mr. John Hardy of London, Dr. Georg Kugler of Vienna, Mr. Olaf Lemke of Berlin and Dr. Erich Schleier, also of Berlin.

I am indebted to Mr. von Abercron of Munich for many references as well as for help in gathering the illustrations, as I am to Mrs. Cailleux (Paris), Dr. Chiarini (Florence), Mr. von Doderer (Stockdorf), Mr. Eggeling (Berlin), Dr. Eickemeier (Munich), Dr. Ewald (Stuttgart), Dr. Himmelheber (Munich), Mr. Laing (London), Dr. Keller (Vienna), Dr. Marzocchi (Bologna), Mr. Merrington (London), Dr. Moschini (Venice), Mr. Pfefferle (Munich), Dr. Saran (Feldafing), Mrs. Shapley (Washington), Dr. von Sonnenburg (Munich), Mr. Gibson (London), Dr. Wütherich (Zurich), as well as the staff of the Framing Department of the National Gallery, London.

My thanks go to the staff of the press for their patience and readiness to accommodate my changing desires.

Claus Grimm

For their help in providing photographs, I gratefully acknowledge the help of Morris H. Heckscher, Paul W. Dull, Jr., Kennedy Galleries, Inc., the Cleveland Museum of Art, the Frick Collection, the Metropolitan Museum of Art, the Museum of Fine Arts in Springfield, Mass., and the Rijksbureau voor Kunsthistorische Dokumentatie, the Hague.

George Szabo

Glossary of Special Terms

Archivolt
The forward face of a round arch. In relation to the edicule frames, it is used to designate the forward face of the over-topping cornice, to the extent that this consists of an arch or of several segments of an arch; they are frequently richly ornamented.

Azure, see Stain.

Blind Frame
The invisible structural base. This frame, double thick to the rear, is frequently of poor quality wood. In the 16th century the practice was adopted of sawing the ornamentation out of a variety of veneers and gluing this onto the wood of the blind frame. Previously it had been customary to attach the ornamentation, cut from more valuable wood, and the profile trim to the blind frame. To the extent that the frame profile consisted purely of trim strips glued to the picture panel—as was the case with many frames of the 14th and 15th centuries and with Art Nouveau—the structure of the picture panel and the blind frame were one and the same.

Bole
Aluminum silicate with ferric hydroxide. This fine-grained finishing substance makes it possible to prepare very smooth surfaces. For glossy gilding and as a base for painting, these qualities are very important. In the gilding technique, bole colors of yellow, white, red, brown, blue and black are used. Yellow and red bole colors are to be found in all epochs, black bole having been used in the Gothic era. In the 19th century there was a preference for brown, blue and black bole. Black bole polish was the choice in silver applications. The color of the base finished by bole affects the gilding or silvering by giving it a warmer or colder tone.

Brush Gilding
The application of gold bronze.

Bulk Gold
A combination of glue, chalk and rosin. This mass is pressed into negative forms or molds, and then fastened onto the frame surface with glue. Like stucco, it was much used in Italy in the Baroque period, in England in the 18th century and in the Baroque imitations of the 19th century. Ornamentation (especially corner ornamentation) is created from bulk gold as well as from gypsum in so-called "gypsum foundries," and then glued onto the wood frames.

"Canaletto" Frames, see page 10.

Cartouche
A decorative member composed of a shield-shaped inner piece with a surrounding frame. The latter can be composed of rolled, ribbon, leaf, muscled or other structural forms. Cartouches are first encountered in elegant manneristic frames, later as middle or corner ornaments in French Baroque frames.

Chip Carving
Carried out with notching tools or knives or an engraver, an ornamental decoration cut into a flat surface, generally with a very uniform appearance. Likewise to be found in subdued forms in which the meaning is suggestive, as in the case of flat frames (Ill. 147).

Construction, Construction Keys
Of frames, can be explained in terms of the preparation and joining of a few elements. The material (wood) is worked to accommodate the general form and the cohesion of the frame structure. In relation to the degree of refinement of the surface effect and the ornamental decoration, attached pieces are added to the forward-facing or visible side, with corresponding preparation procedures. Along with the type of wood used, the construction characteristics of the blind frame reveal differentiating

qualities of regional origin. Historical criteria derive, however, solely from the general differences separating cruder and more uneven preparatory work prior to the 19th century. Italian, Spanish and German blind frames are frequently lap jointed, rarely miter cut; French and English frames are frequently miter cut and wedged (also double wedged, see Dovetail Joint). The preparatory work exhibits noteworthy differences; in the case of German frames, the rear side is planed smooth; in Italian frames the planing is less complete; and planing is scarcely evident in Spanish frames, which are correspondingly rough. The attaching of profiles and ornamentation is accomplished mostly by extensive gluing. Only in the case of frames from the Alpine lands does one find material-saving construction methods using ridges and cavities.

Cuff

Flat, mostly bright-colored or golden intervening strip between the frame profile and the surface of the picture. This device, intended originally as a mere assist to the format, became a style of its own in the 19th century.

Cymatium

Derived from the Greek, *kyma,* "wave," a decorative trim piece composed of stylized leaf forms. The most common type on frames is the so-called "Ionic Cymatium," the "Egg-and-Dart," a convex decorative trim piece which on one or both outside edges is terminated by a string of pearls (Astralagos). The plastic themes on the trim piece have alternating egg-shaped and dart-shaped forms. They are set at right angles to the direction of the trim piece.

Dovetail Joint

A flat double arrow cut with wings which are broader on the outside. This is set into a miter corner on the rear side of a frame at the time of gluing. Cross pieces can be used for the same purpose.

Drip Cap

The under edge of a Gothic frame pitched at a sharp angle toward the outside. This form comes from architecture and has its model in window trim, in which the run-off of water is insured by an angled edge piece.

Edicule Frames

Aedikula is Latin for "small temple." It refers to a structure of columns (or flat columns or pilasters) capped by an architrave and a cornice as entablature. This form, stemming from classical antiquity, had already been adopted in Italy and southern France as early as the Middle Ages to provide a framing for doorways, windows and niches; since the Renaissance it has been used world-wide particularly for altars and cemetery memorials. Italian picture frames of the 15th and 16th centuries, especially those part of large altar structures, are edicule constructions with rich variations rung on the main structural theme. The cornice can rise to a peak and the architrave can be intermittent or in some cases reduced to a mere enlargement of the mass of the column capital.

Engraving

A decorative technique used on the surface of the frame. Ornamental design is cut into the gesso base with pointed instruments (engraving hook, prick punch).

Etching

A scratching procedure mostly used for ornamentation. By this method a wooden pencil-like instrument is used to remove color which had been applied to a polished gold background. The richest examples of this technique are to be found in works of the Italian Renaissance.

Flame Trim

Also called "Rumpel" trim, these are corrugated trim pieces. On two uniformly arced, parallel metal strips, a negative metal profile is affixed whose frequent movement this way and that brings out the wave-like surface of the trim. At the latest, since the 17th century, molding planes and hand-operated eccentric milling devices have been used to create this effect.

Flat Frames

A type in which the frame is created by a flat band laid around the picture and in some cases separated from it by nothing more than a profile on the inner and outer edges. The front facing can, however, be decoratively formed. Still, in contrast to profile frames, these have no marked elevation or depression in them, but remain basically fixed on the level of the picture itself.

Foliation

The leaf-like fitting together of a blind frame, whose overlapping layers hold the boards together. This technique gives the greatest possible rigidity to a frame.

Frame Core

The inner frame, in contrast to the decorative features attached around the outside.

Gesso Base

The glue and chalk binder used to achieve the preparation, the filling and isolation of the surface. Instead of chalk, gypsum was used in Italy; thus "Bologna gesso" is fully mixed gypsum and glue. All gold bases and color foundations on wood require a gesso base. This base preparation is carried through in several layers.

Glazing

For covering small formats (miniatures, religious representations to be kissed), rock crystal or horn glass has been used since the Middle Ages; in the smallest format, precious stones. Glazing of larger formats is first detectable in the 17th century (an example is the glazed original frame of a drawing by de Bodt, around 1695, formerly in the copper engraving collection, Berlin). The greater numbers of.

and the hanging of pastel pictures in the 18th century was dependent on glass-making technology. In the 19th and early 20th centuries, glazing was introduced into many old picture frames in museums.

Gold Bronze
A cheaper substitute for gold. Pulverized tin is mixed with copper, a fluid binder is added and the result is applied and polished (hence the designation, "polished bronze"). This technique was frequently employed in the Art Nouveau period.

Gold Leaf
Very thin hammered gold. The various "leaves" were in earlier periods as thin as .001mm; today they have a thickness of .000125.

Gold Leaf Gilding
The application technique for gold leaf. This has not changed since the Middle Ages. The gold, cut into different sizes, is applied to the base, which has been sized and treated with bole, and then polished (Fig. 2). In the case of medieval pictures, which were placed in the frame prior to the painting (this was the practice up to the early 16th century), the gilding preceded the execution of the painting.

Gold Metal
Copper-tin alloys, which today, in modern frame gilding, are used as a substitute for gold in oil gilding.

Grooves, Spinal Grooves, Grooved Trim
These serve as linkage for frame parts and frame edges. The terms refer to sloping, U-shaped indentations in wood, which imitate the corresponding negative form of the appropriate "spring," that is, of the edge of the picture. Thus the Gothic panel pictures were firmly set into a corresponding groove of the frames surrounding them. Spinal grooves have a trapezoidal form in cross-section and use the grooved trim as "spring."

Guilloching
The creation of complex geometric designs; occasionally the term is used for the creation of flame trim.

Keel Arc
A bowed form resembling, in plain view, the keel of a ship, composed of segments of a circle, with convex and concave curvature. The term is used for the cap portion of Gothic altar framing.

"Lely" Frames see page 10.

Louis XIII
The style prevailing during the reign of Louis XIII in France (1601-1643). It took up the architectonic structure of the Italian Renaissance frames and was characterized by a marked emphasis on the profile.

Louis XIV
The style prevailing during the reign of the "Sun King," Louis XIV, in France (1643-1715). The leading role of the court, and the standing of the art of interior decoration imitated in the rest of Europe, justifies the use of the reigns of the French kings as style designations.

Louis XV
The style prevailing during the reign of Louis XV in France (1723-1774). This style, characterized by Rococo ornamentation and voluminous curves, began to give way as early as the '50s to classical elements, which increased in the Transition style toward the reign of Louis XVI. In England the Louis XV style coincided with that of George II (reign of the English king George II, 1727-1760).

Louis XVI
The style prevailing under Louis XVI (1774-1792), which formed the transition to classicism. In Germany it corresponded to the Rococo style. The high point of this muted early classicism came in the late '60s and the '70s.

Luster Finish
A technique in use since the Renaissance to achieve a metallic effect in color. In this technique, transparent color paint is applied like glass to a silver base. The most frequently used colors are red (called "dragon blood red"), yellow, green and blue. As a substitute for gold one frequently encounters "luster gilding." On a polished flat silver base, yellow luster coloration is applied. The combination of characteristics produces an effect similar to that of polished gilding. Luster gilding is particularly used to provide color differentiation of ornamental parts on frames.

"Lutma" Frames, see page 10.

"Maratta" Frames, see page 10.

Marbling
This is accomplished by means of the application of color either in a strip or in clumps with brush, sponge or linen rags. In frames one first encounters marbling with Jan van Eyck; it is very common in the late Renaissance, and in the Baroque and Rococo styles.

"Marchesi" Frames, see page 10.

Masks
Ornamentally reconstructed mask forms are to be found in the Italian Renaissance both on the surface and on the corners of frames.

Mat Gold, Mat Gilding
A technique in which—as opposed to that employed for gleaming gold—the surface is not polished. Even in this case gold leaf is used, but the base is more extensively prepared with sizing. Mat gold is frequently used on the same frame as gleaming gold, as a contrast to it.

Material
That of picture frames is normally wood. In exceptional cases it can be metal (bronze, iron, silver or gold) or ceramics (stoneware or china). Additions attached to the frame skeleton can be in a variety of materials: precious stones, semi-precious stones, corals including all kinds of plant and animal materials, glass, metal, stucco and papier-mâché.

Miniature Framing
Framing corresponding to small format. With the exception of closed forms used for likeness and devotional representations (wooden boxes, closing etuis, lockets), miniature framing follows the patterns of large picture frames. Adapted to smaller format, this technique prefers metal and metallic parts for the skeleton and for the ornamental parts.

Mortising
The binding together of two wood pieces with wooden dowels, or with triangular-shaped corner binders.

Ogee
A round rod combined with a hollow rod. This S-shaped profile, bending either backward or forward, is employed as a regular element in frames for molding or as a base.

Oil Gilding
This begins with a base similar to that for gleaming gold. Shellac is applied to isolate the base (gesso) and the surface is then painted with a mixture (binder oil). The gold is laid on this elastic, slowly drying binder and pressed in. The surface effect is mat.

Papier-mâché
A mass of paper, soaked in water until mush, with the addition of glue, starch and gypsum. This was used in the 18th century for the creation of ornamental strips, which in their dried state could then be gilded.

Pastiglia
A mass containing gypsum, which has been used in Italy since the Middle Ages for the decoration of furniture. It is mostly applied to lightly curved profiles; by the use of a mold it can be given ornamental and figure-like shapes. On frames, pastiglia surfaces are stained with color and—judging by the preserved specimens—frequently gilded. The richest examples of pastiglia ornamentation are to be found in the Venetian frames around 1500.

Pebbling
One of the oldest techniques for decorating a gilded surface—by means of metal punches—whose working surface is characterized by various negative forms (points, circles, lines).

Pilaster
A flat half-column or a flat, impressed square piping. This architectonic form is frequently used in Renaissance frames. In contrast to the pilaster strip, it possesses both pedestal and capital.

Pipe Cut
A hollow, tube-like cut, which runs at right angles to the frame profile. Particularly among the manneristic and the classicistic frames of the 19th century is this form readily found.

Polish
Smoothing procedure using agate, by which gold is brought to a high polish.

Polish Gilding, see **Bole.**

Profile, Profiling
The dynamic, forward or backward-bending, plastically formed forward surface of a trim piece. It is produced by hand-planed trim pieces or by special profile planes.

Profile Frames, see **Trim Frames.**

Rabbet or Groove
In frames, the rearward fastening holding the picture. In framing of the late Middle Ages the picture panels, if they were not fitted into a surrounding grooved piece prior to the addition of the framing material proper, were attached to the frame by a corresponding rabbet or groove strip at the rear.

Regency
The style prevailing in France during the Regency of Philippe of Orleans (1715-1723). It constitutes the transitional form between the leaf and branch ornamentation of the Louis XIV style to the more playful Rococo of the Louis XV period. Identifying characteristics are the preference for geometric, flat ornamentation. Strap work is an important structural element. The Regency forms link objective decorative designs (leaves, tendrils, architectonic elements) through symmetrically repeated bands of ribbon. From the middle of the '30s onward the expressive forms and the ornamental concepts are inextricably interwoven: from the time when this mixed form appears the Rococo begins, that is, the Louis XV style. The period in England corresponding to the Regency is that of George I (1714-1727).

Rib, Ribbing
The gutter-like indentation of a backward-bending profile.

Rods
Profile rods, separately prepared for all profile-using frames and subsequently glued on. Major types are the egg-and-dart (cymatium), spiral rod (turned rod), leaf rod and quarter rod.

"Salvator Rosa" Frames, see page 10.

Sanding
The application of fine-grain, sieved sand to the frame surface. The corresponding sections are painted with liquid glue, which causes the sand sifted onto them to adhere. After drying, a thin gesso base can be applied and on top of this the gilding. This technique was much used, particularly in English and French frames of the 18th century.

"Sansovino" Frames, see page 10.

Scaffolding and **Structural Wood**, see **Blind Frame.**

Shoelace Trim or **String Trim**
This consists of "pearls" of wood or gilded material which are strung on a line. They are attached to the frame profile prior to the base preparation and treated together with this latter.

Silvering
Basically the same technique as gilding.

Spine Trim

Used particularly in the case of wide frames of large format, in order to hold the miter corners together in the face of the wood's natural tendency to shrink. The spinal groove at right angles to the miter corner has a trapezoidal form, narrower at the top.

Spring Mitering

This is to be found as a structural strengthening of the corners cut in miter form, particularly in English frames. In the simplest form the corners, after gluing, are cut out or beveled toward the rear, and covered over with a wooden corner piece or "spring" which is glued on. Its wood grain runs at right angles to that of the side-piece of the frame. In the case of thick frames, it is possible to find several parallel "springs" one on top of another and countersunk in the wood.

Stain, Staining

The tinting of the wood, thus changing the color character and obscuring defects. Staining can also designate the toning down of the gilding. The particular color effect is mostly achieved by means of a water stain. Prior to the 19th century azure (copper carbonate) was the primary substance used for staining. The original form of stain was single-shade azure with little penetration. The shading colors were originally earth colors (earth-colored shading). Besides water stains, alcohol stains were used, and since the 19th century, soluble glass stains. The wax stains which affect only the surface belong to more recent times.

Stucco Frames

Simpler and cheaper forms of plastically decorated frames. As early as the Baroque period, the art world of many countries produced a rich selection of stucco decoration on frames, which then became the normal form of ornamental and figured decoration in the 19th century. A particular advantage of stucco is the possibility of applying this over several profiles. In contrast to hand-cut frames, these forms produced with molds lend themselves to mass production. Stucco, made from a combination of stucco gypsum and liquid glue, is a material which can readily be manipulated.

"Sunderland" Frames, see page 10.

Tabernacle Frames

These derive their designation from their resemblance to the face side of a tabernacle. Tabernacle or Ciborium are the terms used for the container for the blessed bread, the host. The Ciborium, since the Middle Ages, has been chiefly made of metal. It consists of a base or pedestal, a container body and a cover or crown. The features of tabernacle frames which correspond to this are the special, reinforced pedestal, and the emphasized crown in relation to the central container for the picture, which can consist both of bearing pilasters on the side and bearing joists, as well as of frame profiles which surround all sides. Set against the edicule type used in large

formats, the tabernacle form is smaller. The former is, in contrast to the latter, a simplified device. Late manifestations of the tabernacle form are characterized by the disappearance of the pedestal and the simplification of the crown to a horizontal stringer. In the central zone of the picture housing, the form of a uniform flat or profile frame is detectable.

Tondo

The term means "round picture," a very popular form in the second half of the 15th century. Stimulated by the wreath frames of majolica, as they were produced in the della Robbia reliefs, comparable picture frames were carved from wood.

Toothed Cut

A form of the frieze, thus a structural strip, which is linked by an equal sequence of three- or four-cornered slanted "teeth."

Transition

Transitional phase from the Louis XV style to that of Louis XVI, in which the free curves of the ornamentation are tied into solid lines. A preferred type among frames is the heavily emphasized swinging ribbon used as exterior delimitation of the decorative zone.

Trim, Profile Trim

A board planed into profile form.

Trim Frames

In contrast to the flat surface frames, a frame with a profiled leading edge, that is, viewed in cross-section from the inside out, a frontispiece with plastic ascending or descending gradations.

Veneering

Covering over a structural or blind wood form with a surface of fine cabinet wood. Bent veneer pieces are dampened and, after gluing, held in shape with heavy sacks of sand. Assorted woods are used for veneer work. Since the late Renaissance it has been primarily in northern Europe that the majority of flat frame profiles have had such cover pieces of more elegant material attached to them. Even ornamentation and decorative inlay pieces have been attached using the veneer technique, however this is more often the case with mirror frames than with picture frames. In Holland and in the Alpine lands particularly, rich veneer work is to be found from the 17th century onward, sometimes with alternating ornamentation within the profile sequence. Prior to the 19th century, veneer was hand cut.

Wood

With the exception of a few picture frames of metal or ceramics, the basic structural material of picture frames is wood, to which is attached assorted decorative additions of wood, metal, ivory, tortoise shell and stucco. According to the prevailing kinds of wood used, different European countries put together different combinations of blind frame, profile and ornamentation. In England, Holland, Germany and Austria the wood choice as material for the blind frame was overwhelmingly softwood (spruce or fir), while in France oak was typical. In Italy softwoods were frequently used, occasionally basswood, mostly poplar. In Russia blind frames of birch were typical. The attached profile pieces were, in Holland and Germany, made of nut and fruit woods, but also some made of spruce can be found; in France they were of oak and in Italy of poplar, pine and nut wood. The carved ornamentation was frequently of the same wood as the profile, occasionally however of material which was particularly easy to work, such as poplar or basswood. The dark veneer of the Dutch frames was of ebony. In similar frames in the Alpine countries, it was of pearwood, which because of its fine grain was used as a substitute for ebony.

Bibliography

History and Philosophy of Art

Semper, G. *Der Stil,* Munich 1863.
Falke, J. von. *Ästhetik des Kunstgewerbes,* Stuttgart 1883.
Burckhardt, J. "Das Altarbild," *Beiträge zur Kunstgeschichte von Italien,* Basel 1930 (Reprint).
Dollmayer, H. "Alte Bilderrahmen," *Die Kunst für Alle* 13, 1898.
Marshall, H. "Zur Ästhetik und Geschichte des Rahmens," *Universum* 16, 1898.
Simmel, G. "Der Bilderrahmen," *Tag,* No. 54, 1902.
Everth, E. *Der Bilderrahmen als ästhetischer Ausdruck von Schutzfunktionen,* Leipzig 1904.
Schmarsow, A. *Grundbegriffe der Kunstwissenschaft,* Leipzig 1905.
Sander, G. *Georg Sanders Lehrbuch für den Einrahmer,* Osnabrück 1924.
Ayrshire, W. "The Philosophy of the Picture Frame," *International Studlo,* New York, June 1926.
Tsudzima, T. "Die Rahmenlosigkeit des japanischen Kunststils," *Zeitschrift für Ästhetik und allgemeine Kunstwissenschaft,* 1928.
Foth, M. "Wie rahmen wir unsere Bilder?" *Zeitschrift für Psychologie und Physiologie der Sinnesorgane, Zeitschrift für Psychologie,* vol. 41, 2 and 3.
Hartlaub, G. *Zauber des Spiegels,* Munich 1951.
Homann-Wedeking, E. "Die Entstehung der abendländischen Bildform," *Studies presented to David M. Robinson,* II, St. Louis, 1953.
Ortega y Gasset "Meditationen über den Rahmen," *Über die Liebe,* Stuttgart 1954.
White, J. *The Birth and Rebirth of Pictorial Space,* London 1957.
Seckler, D.G. "The Art of Framing," *Art in America,* Spring 1958.
Brandi, C. "Togliere o conservare le cornici come problema di restauro," *Bolletino dell'Instituto Centrale del Restauro* 36, 1958.
Kamphausen, A. "Bilderrahmen, ein museales Thema," *Festschrift für Richard Sedlmaier,* Lübeck 1960.

Schneckenburger, M. "Das Bildformat. Geschichte und künstlerische Bedeutung vom Mittelalter bis zum Rokoko." (Dissertation), Tübingen 1973.

Sociology

Lerner-Lehmkuhl, H. *Zur Struktur und Geschichte des Florentiner Kunstmarktes im 15. Jahrhundert,* Münster 1936.
Davies, M. *Paintings and Drawings on the Backs of National Gallery Pictures,* London 1946.
Keller, H. "Der Flügelaltar als Reliquienschrein," *Studien zur Geschichte der europäischen Plastik,* Munich 1965, pp.125-144.
Wills, G. *English Looking Glasses. A study of the glass, frames and makers, 1670-1820,* London 1965.
Huth, H. *Künstler und Werkstatt der Spägotik,* Darmstadt 1967.
Warnke, M. "Italienische Bildtabernakel bis zum Frühbarock," *Münchner Jahrbuch der bildenden Kunst* 1968, p.61ff.
Honour, H. *The Social History of Decorative Arts,* London 1968.
Honour, H. *Cabinet Makers and Furniture Designers,* London 1969.
White, J. "Carpentry and Design in Duccio's Workshop: the London and Boston triptychs," *Journal of the Warburg and Courtauld Institute* 1973.
Koller, M. "Fassung und Fassmaler an Barockaltären," *Maltechnik/Restauro* 1976, p.157ff.

Studies of Ornament and Furniture

Chippendale, T. *The Gentleman and Cabinet-Makers Director,* London 1754[1], 1759[2], 1762[3], (Reprint) New York 1938.
Ince and Mayhew. *The Universal System of Household Furniture,* London, ca. 1762.
Lock, M. *New Book of Pier Frames,* Ovals, Gerandoles, Tables, etc.,* London 1769.
Dohme, R. *Möbel aus den Kgl. Schlössern Berlin und Potsdam,* Berlin 1866.
Bode, W. von. *Hausmöbel der Renaissance, (Spiegelrahmen),* (Monographien des Kunstgewerbes 6), Leipzig n.d.
Schidlof, L. *Die Bildnisminiatur in Frankreich,* Vienna/Leipzig 1911.
Ferrari, G. *Il legno e la mobilia,* Milan, n.d.
Harvard, H. *Dictionnaire de l'ameublement et de la décoration,* I, Paris, n.d.
Jessen, P. *Meister des Ornamentstichs,* 2 vols., Berlin 1921.
de Jonge, C.H. *Holländ. Möbel und Raumkunst 1650-1780,* (Bauformen-Bibliothek 13), Stuttgart (1922).
Schottmüller, F. *Wohnungskultur und Möbel der italienischen Renaissance,* (Bauformen-Bibliothek 13), Stuttgart 1922.
Macquoid, P. and Edwards, R. *Dictionary of English Furniture,* London 1928.
Midana, A. *L'Arte del legno in Piemonte,* Turin n.d.
Ricci, S. de. *Louis XIV und Régence,* (Bauformen-Bibliothek 26), Stuttgart 1929.
Zülch, W.K. Entstehung des Ohrmuschelstils, Heidelberg 1932.
Schwarz, H. "Das Bandelwerk." (Dissertation), Vienna 1950.
Mariacher, G. *Specchiere italiane e cornici da specchio del XV al XVI secolo,* Milan 1953.
Comte de Salverte. *Les ébénistes du XVIIIe siècle,* Paris 1962[5].
Fowler, J. and Cornforth, J. *English Decoration in the 18th Century,* London 1974.

Collections of Models and Essays Pertaining to the History of Frames

Guerimet, A. *Collection de cadres scultés des tableaux du Musée du*

Louvre et du Musée de l'Union Central des Arts Décoratifs, Paris 189?.

Falke, J. von. *Sammlungen des K.K. Österreichischen Museums für Kunst und Industrie (Abt. Rahmen),* Vienna 1892.

Lessing, J. *Vorbilderhefte aus dem Kgl. Kunstgewerbemuseum in Berlin,* 1-4 and 20, 1888-1895, Berlin 1895.

Bösch, H. *Bilder- und Spiegelrahmen von A. Dürer bis zum Rokoko,* Leipzig 1897.

Guggenheim, A. *Le cornici italiane della metà del secolo XV. allo scorcio del sec. XVI.,* Milan 1897.

Bode, W. von. "Bilderrahmen in alter und neuer Zeit," *Pan IV,* 1898.

Bock, E. *Florentinische und venezianische Bilderrahmen,* Munich 1902.

Bode, W. von. "Ausstellung der Gemälde im K. Fr. Museum mit altem Rahmen," *Amtliche Berichte der Berliner Museen* 33, 1912.

Cadres et Bordures des Tableaux de la fin du XVIe siècle au Premiere Empire, A. Calvas, ed., Paris (1912).

Bode, W. von. "Rahmen und Sockel in Italien zur Zeit der Renaissance," *Kunst und Künstler* 17, 1918/19.

Martin, W. *Altholländische Bilder,* Berlin 1921.

Bode, W. von. "Antike Rahmen," Exhibition Künstlerhaus, Berlin 1929.

Braun, J. *Der christliche Altar,* Munich 1924.

Ellwood, G.M. and Braun, A.A. "Italian Frames of the Fifteenth and Sixteenth Centuries," *Connoisseur* LXXXIII, 1929.

Roche, S. *Cadres français et étrangers du XVe au XVIIIe siècle,* Paris 1931.

Hauptmann, M. *Der Tondo,* Frankfurt a.M. 1936.

Le Cadre published by "Le Cadre" Société anonyme, Brussels n.d.

Morazzoni, G. *Le cornici veneziane,* Milan n.d. (ca. 1940 and ca. 1954).

Köllmann, E. "Bilderrahmen," *Reallexikon zur Deutschen Kunstgeschichte* II, Stuttgart 1948.

Ehlich, Werner. "Zur Entstehung des antiken Bilderrahmens," *Zeitschrift für Kunst IV,* 1950.

Seckel, C. "Betrachtungen zur Geschichte des Bilderrahmens," *Kunsthandel* (Heidelberg), April 1951, May 1951, June 1951, July 1951.

Morazzoni, G. *Le cornici bolognesi,* Milan 1953.

Steinbrucker, C. "Kurzbeiträge," *Kunsthandel* (Heidelberg), Sept. 1953, Nov. 1956, Jan. 1957.

Schmidt, I. "Der gotische Bilderrahmen in Deutschland und den Niederlanden." (Dissertation), Freiburg i.Br. 1954.

Ehlich, W. *Bild und Rahmen im Altertum. Die Geschichte des Bilderrahmens,* Leipzig 1955.

Ehlich, W. "Tafelbildrahmung im Altertum," *Forschungen und Fortschritte* 29, 1955.

Stange, A. and Cremer, L. *Alte Bilderrahmen,* Darmstadt 1958.

Heydenryk, H. *The Art and History of Frames. An inquiry into the enhancement of paintings,* New York 1963.

Cämmerer-George, M. *Die Rahmung der toskanischen Altarbilder im Trecento,* Strasbourg 1966.

van Thiel, P.J.J. "Hollandse lijsten van balein," *Miscellanea I.Q. van Regteren Altena,* Amsterdam 1969.

Individual Artists and Works

Tietze, H. "Der Rahmen von Dürers Allerheiligenbild," *Pantheon* VIII, 1931.

Covi, D. "A XVIth Century Italian Altarpiece," *Bulletin of the Metropolitan Museum of Art,* Jan. 1958.

Möller, L. "Ein niederländischer Bilderrahmen aus dem 17. Jahrhundert," *Jahrbuch der Hamburger Kunstsammlungen* 7, 1962.

van Molle, F. "Identification d'un portrait de Gilles Joye attribué à Memlinc," Brussels 1960.

Windisch-Graetz, F. "Die Entstehungsgeschichte des Hochaltars vom Sonntagberg und die Marmorengel von Johann Christoph Schletterer," *Alte und moderne Kunst* 1963, p.16ff.

Green, D. *Grinling Gibbons,* London 1964.

Crinò, A.M. "An unpublished document on the frame of Elsheimers tabernacle," *Burlington Magazine* 1965, p.575.

Behling, L. "Das italienische Pflanzenbild um 1400, zum Wesen des pflanzlichen Dekors auf dem Epiphaniasbild des Gentile da Fabriano in den Uffizien," *Pantheon* 1966, pp. 347-359.

Cämmerer-George, M. "Eine italienische Wurzel in der Rahmen-Idee Jan van Eycks," *Kunstgeschichtliche Studien für Kurt Bauch,* Munich/Berlin 1967, pp.69-76.

Verbeek, H. "De houtsnijder Hermanus van Arnhem," *Bulletin van het Rijksmuseum,* Amsterdam, March 1968 and June 1968.

White, J. "Measurement, design and carpentry in Duccio's Maestà," *The Art Bulletin* 1973, p.334ff. and p.547ff.

Stewart, J.D. "New Light on the Early Career of Grinling Gibbons," *Burlington Magazine* 1976, p.508ff.

Technical and Scientific Research

Coremans, P. "L'agneau mystique au laboratoire," *Les Primitifs Flamands* III, 2., Antwerp 1953.

Marette, J. *Connaissance des Primitifs par l'étude du bois,* Paris 1961.

Straub, R.E. "Einige technologische

Untersuchungen am Tiefenbronner Magdalenenaltar des Lukas Moser," *Jahrbuch der Staatlichen Kunstsammlungen in Baden-Württemberg,* VII, 1970.

Richter, E.L. "Zur Rekonstruktion des Tiefenbronner Magdalenenaltars," *Pantheon* 30, 1972.

van Asperen de Boer, J.R.J. "A Technical Examination of the Frame of Engelbrechtzs's 'Crucifixion' and some other 16th-Century Frames," *Nederlands Kunsthistorisch Jaarboek* 26, 1975.

Grosser, D. "Holzanatomische Untersuchungen der italienischen Rahmen der Alten Pinakothek München" (unveröffentlichte Arbeit, *Italienische Bilderrahmen des 14.-18. Jahrhunderts,* Munich 1976).

Germann, P. "Die Rahmen der Jahreszeitenreliefs von Soldani im Bayerischen Nationalmuseum München," *Maltechnik/Restauro* 1978, p.116ff.

Catalogues

Sale de Biron, Paris 1914.

Catalogue de l'Exposition du cadre ancien à la Galerie L. Sambon, Paris 1924.

Catalogue of English Furniture and Woodwork in the Victoria and Albert-Museum, vol. 3, London 1927.

Antike Rahmen im Künstlerhaus Berlin, May-June 1929.

Sale Böhler, *Kunstwerke aus dem Besitz der Staatl. Museen Berlin,* Munich 1937.

Mostra del Barocco Piemontese, 2 vols. Torino 1963.

Les Primitifs de Boheme, Brussels 1966.

Holländische Gemälde aus französischen Museen, Amsterdam 1971.

Victorian and Edwardian Decorative Art. The Handley-Read Collection, London 1972.

Die Bildhauerfamilie Schwanthaler 1633-1848, Stift Reichersberg 1974.

Gli ultimi Medici—il tardo barocco a firenze, 1670-1743, Florence 1975.

Mary Beale—exhibition 1975, London, Geffrye-Museum.

Het Symbolisme in Europa, Rotterdam 1975.

Porträtgalerie zur Geschichte Österreichs von 1400 bis 1800, Vienna, Kunsthistorisches Museum 1976.

Italienische Bilderrahmen des 14.-18. Jahrhunderts, Alte Pinakothek, Munich 1976.

Barocke Malerei aus den Anden, 2 vols., Düsseldorf 1977.

Fig. 1.   Thomas Chippendale (c.1709-79). Design inscribed "picture frame," c.1750. *London, Victoria and Albert Museum.*

Origin and Development of Picture Frames

This book is an introduction to the history of picture frames. The history of painting has been told from many points of view, but for a general survey of the epochs in frame making there are few starting points. This is not due to chance, for the forms in which picture frames have appeared permit no simple classification. Should they be arranged according to the styles of painting or according to the styles of furniture?

Functionally they belong to both domains: they mark off limits, integrate or provide a link between the picture and the surrounding room.

Even the notions of what a picture is and what it should represent have changed in the course of time, and this applies also to what is demanded of the "furnishing," that is, the character and arrangement of the contents of a room as a whole.

Boundaries, enclosures, margins, end strips, borders—these are the means commonly used in the various cultures in order to fix, to emphasize and, in the widest sense, to set off a field of accentuated form. Yet nowhere outside European culture have these auxiliary functions been worked out in such detail and in such a variety of forms. Nowhere else has there evolved an individual class of handicraft creations, sculpturally modeled and with precious settings; creations that after all were restricted only in their format, but which in their forms of expression became independent. This special development is closely connected with another unique cultural creation, the *illusionistic panel painting.*

It must be realized that the movable picture hanging on the wall of an interior room first emerged at the beginning of modern times. It became customary in middle-class living rooms only from the 17th century onward. Rooms in the Middle Ages were decorated with wall paintings, wall facings and tapestry. Although toward the close of the Middle Ages the art of wall painting was highly developed, painting techniques and creative methods nevertheless reached their full development only on the detached panels that could be painted in the artist's studio, independent of the conditions at the place where they would be set up later (the expression "easel picture" also comes from this). Since the 12th century we have been acquainted with panels set up free-standing on altars; as development proceeded these were displaced by constantly richer and bigger superstructures. In the middle of the 13th century there arose the altar picture in a number of parts, in which the sculptured or painted decorative panels were arranged in a kind of architectural casing. Their richest form is represented by the polyptychs of the end of the 15th and the beginning of the 16th centuries. With their flat framing the various painted altar panels can be regarded as precursors of the modern panel painting.

With the transfer of these pictures to walls and with the removal of their restriction to a church setting with its fixed and predetermined contents, the ground was prepared for modern esthetic concepts. Beyond their symbolic references, the paintings demand increasing attention to their quite special "artistic" message. This new intrinsic value differentiates the perceptive realism of the picture panels from the manner in which they were usually looked at up to then. Not only was there an appreciation of the subtlety achieved in the reproduction of nature, but by means of a visionary description of the laws of nature and of the forces underlying pure existence: from the 15th century onward the "artists" and their pictures received a higher status in the circle of the "Arts and Sciences," in the recognized system of knowledge and abilities. The new significance of the panels determines the character of the frames, which only from here onward are free from the restriction to liturgical functions. Thus, regarded historically, this type of frame has its start with the onset of modern times. What earlier examples were intended to signify can illustrate the preliminary stages, which, however, can be termed "picture frames" only in a very limited sense.

The development of the picture frame did not lie simply in the creation of a new device that rapidly became accepted as a matter of course and as seemingly valid forever. The retreat of certain historical forms of picture and frame cannot escape the notice of the attentive observer of modern home decor. It is not only that commercial art and art prints are displacing the oil painting from living rooms, but also that in many less official rooms posters and other types of pictures are merely stuck or clipped or pinned on or fastened between plain sheets of glass. Often only a decorative wallpaper or piece of tapestry has taken the place of the former wealth of pictures in the living room, not to speak of the bareness of modern churches or of secular rooms for important non-religious functions.

An observation of this kind stands in only apparent contradiction to the fact that frames are being collected more than ever, both with and without pictures (or as mirror frames), that they can be found in expensive suites of furniture and are already being exhibited in museums as independent works of art. Today, in contrast to a period as recent as the mid-nineteenth century, there is no longer an obligatory style of interior decoration calling for uniform principles of framing—whether for the public gallery or the private room. There are no longer any originally creative frame makers, from whom suitable designs could be ordered, more or less magnificent. There are instead restorers, who in one case or the other can copy some carving or compose something, but even they are having difficulty in finding young talent to carry on their work. And all

presentations of splendid and outstanding frames—whether in museums or in private houses—exhibit them in their historical uniqueness, in the character of their historical setting—with some damage in contrast to other objects of a different style.

The beauty experienced with old picture frames is fundamentally different from the ideals of present-day production: it bears witness to a kind of historical artistry that can never be repeated. In this respect two different points of view overlap within contemporary furnishing styles: framing designed primarily for holding pictures is conceived according to functional criteria, whereas the frames of highly select form remain "historical" and are found only in museums or where historical values are conjured into life, as in imposing ceremonial interiors or with collectors.

This coming to an end of the artistic frame can be explained only through the overall development of the interpretative arts. The significance of images for various life-styles—in the most general sense—has been steadily diminishing since the Middle Ages. The fact that figures and pictures are today only "Art"—and no longer essential objects of daily life—alters the value of their message. Consequently, the more indistinct the functions of pictures became the vaguer became also the boundary-function of the frame, which in the 19th century changed into esthetic furniture. In beautiful uniformity and without individual regard for the respective pictures, the frames of salons and galleries could thus be brought into line with the style of furnishing obligatory at any particular time.

In contrast to the Romantic-Classicistic cultural and educational ideal of "Art," Realism and Impressionism inaugurated a revaluation of what can be formed and is felt from impressions of reality. Now it depended only on the harmony of sense perceptions on the eye of the observer. And finally the creation of form became only a process of directed subjective and highly personal imagination, with all its arbitrariness and inaccessibility. What could be expressed through painting remained within the free play of the psychological mechanisms of projection and interpretation. To mark off its limits an intermediate path to the surrounding surface sufficed. According to the effect intended in each case this could be lighter or darker, a harmonious transition or a glaring separation. Whether for such demarcation one chose, like some Impressionists, old frames painted over (Ill. 417), or, like Seurat and his circle, border strips specially colored (Ill. 418), or else would-be historical or actual historical frames (Ill. 445, 446): it was always a matter of the two-dimensional impression.

Without passing a value judgment it can be stated that paintings today are conceived as two-dimensional developments of a form-substance that is, in fact, artistic, but fictitious compared with normal perception. No one who is accustomed to television and poster walls in his daily life is prepared any longer to share the naive illusion of earlier centuries. The classification as two-dimensional is also made subconsciously and as a matter of course in respect to all other pictures, which today are therefore often framed without discrimination or only according to "esthetic" criteria or even not framed at all. Just for the very reason that an illusion from a prerationalistic era has become foreign to us and because symbolic systems, formerly obligatory, have become buried, the magnificently fashioned frames of earlier times appear to us merely as luxurious and fabulously ornate splendor. On closer study, however, many indications of significance come to light, which make that extravagance more comprehensible.

Frame and "frame" is in each century something different and in the final analysis not comparable. It is some consolation that this problem is more general than many historians are prepared to admit. On scrupulous examination the history of painting or of interior decoration proves to be also a loose correlation of concepts which are only to a limited degree comparable. Just as in those cases where the only feature still in common is brush or hammer, so also the category of the picture frame is fluid. It is to be defined here as the embodiment of a function that in its origin is linked to the painted panel, in contrast to the mirror frame, which is a piece of furniture with quite different artistic aims. The supplementary word "old" picture frames in the title is intended to differentiate the creations of craftsmanship from a later industrial production. In the latter the artistic forms have shrunk to a few standard patterns of easily reproducible quality and somewhat mediocre decorative effect. Here the usefulness of modern framing is not under discussion; rather the character, changing according to periods and the artistic scene, of the rich historical forms is to be described and understood—as a field for the observation of cultural diversity and evidence of a far-reaching historical change.

On the Choice of the Illustrations

In choosing the historical examples an effort was made to cover the widest possible range. In spite of a copious provision of illustrations as a whole, only the main currents of style could be represented. Appraisals inevitably come to mind when individual frames are designated as typical, or they arise of necessity from the nature of the chapters. It was also not possible to obtain data on dimensions for all frames, and it was equally impossible to take account of all varieties. On the contrary, in some main groups only a few artistic forms outstanding for their style are presented in each case. Regional developments are not followed individually, apart from some few sequences of Florentine and French frames. The comparatively detailed research needed for an exact description of the sequence of development has up to now been lacking.

The majority of the illustrations have been so chosen as to combine what is historically typical with an artistic form worked out to a high degree. The representation of the magnificent frame and the decorative frame is in consequence disproportionately high. Detail photographs likewise predominate that especially bring out the ornamental qualities. A documentary record of all individual pieces would also have been desirable; that is, along with detail photographs, a picture of the entire frame should be included as well as several side views. This, however, would have been at the expense of the variety of choice as a whole, and secondly it would have excluded some photographs that were available of details only, or of not quite uniform quality. Good photographs exist only in exceptional cases in museums or in the possession of private owners. For depicting the various settings colored illustrations would certainly have been desirable, but this was outside the bounds of practicable realization.

The Tradition of Historical Frames

Our knowledge of the history of the frame is still in its infancy. The material passed down to us resists historical investigation. There are today many important museums without a single original frame belonging to a picture on exhibition. And so far as old frames are to be found at all, they are frequently adapted, that is, cut down or enlarged; also at times adapted to paintings through changes in their moldings. Many frames have gone through repeated adaptations; they have had the color removed with lye and have been newly mounted, and have wandered through more migrations than the much-traveled pictures. Frames are furniture, are movable property, and in their function of assisting pictures are more subject to wear and tear than the pictures themselves; accordingly they are—with the exception of a few altar forms that have remained unchanged—the most *mobile* of all art objects.

Documentary records about frames are the exception. Only in the case of very few pictures was any reason seen to write a record on the framing, usually taken for granted. Even when this was done, as with the frame for the portrait of the English diarist Pepys (Ill. 238), it is often difficult later to identify the piece described.

It becomes no easier when one attempts today to follow up the more or less well known historical names that are traditionally associated with certain forms of frame. According to the internationally established usage there are indeed "Sansovino" frames (after the master builder and sculptor Jacopo Tatti, named S., 1486-1570), but there is no immediate connection between his designs and the form of frame so designated. Perhaps ornamental forms of the stucco work carried out in the wider workshop circles of the important Venetian architect acted as models, but this is pure conjecture.

One of the few Renaissance artists after whom a small group of frames can be named with good authority is Andrea di Pietro (1480/90-1559), named for his teacher Marchesi. He is mostly referred to as "Marchesi Formigine," after his birthplace Formigine. Altar framings in Bologna churches (Santa Maria dei Servi, San Martino Maggiore) originate from this architect, ornamental sculptor, wood carver, and worker in stucco (Ill. 106, 107). As is the case with Antonio Barile of Siena (1453-1526), who flourished shortly before, the name of the leading master stands for the whole series of workshop products. What is achieved thereby in the way of choir stalls, woodwork and moldings, of portals and picture framing is a selective combination drawing on the various traditions of the art of decoration, and it fascinates through the brilliance of the execution. Other types of frame which arose a little later—this is a striking example of the wealth of interrelationships found in decoration—are named after artists of the most varying genres, as for example the "Maratta" frames (called in Italy "Salvator Rosa" frames) with their English variant of the "Half-Maratta" frames. Their designation links them with the two Roman baroque artists, admittedly without any clear-cut indication being possible of their historical responsibility. The "Lutma" frames stand in general relationship to the ornament designs of the artists in the group of silversmiths around Jan Lutma (about 1584-1669) and Adam van Vianen (about 1569-1627) in the Netherlands. Of the "Lely" and "Canaletto" frames one can say only that they are typical for adorning the pictures of these painters. Most definite is the evidence for the English variant of the Dutch "Lutma" frames, namely the "Sunderland" frames: in 1660-70 during the conversion of his country mansion Althorp Lord Sunderland had his picture gallery—today still preserved in this form—decorated throughout with magnificent frames of this style.

There are no sketches or designs by any of the personalities who have given their names to frames. Drawings and engravings by various other artists have been preserved showing designs for framings and details of ornament. However, up to now, *not one single preliminary draft* has been found that could definitely be assigned to some particular frame as pattern. In a way similar to the products of goldsmiths and workers in stucco, designs for ornament were indeed used, but simply as stimulus in a stream of variations.

As a rule frame makers were craftsmen, mostly members of larger-sized workshops and thus in no way identifiable as individuals. Signed picture frames are rare and are found only very late, namely with the rise in artistic status of the artist-craftsman, of the fine cabinetmaker working for the courts. Here arises a historical problem. Signatures on frames comparable with those on pictures are first met with in the 18th century, for example those of the cabinetmakers Infroit (Ill. 296, 306) and Levert (Ill. 307). Long before that there are of course references and documentary evidence regarding makers of framing, but either these concerned relatively elaborate altar framing, that is, a specially high-ranking sculptural and interior architectural venture, or else the architects that signed were sculptors or architects called in for only one particular order. Even though as early as 1556 the frame maker is named on the predella of the high altar for San Antonio Abate in Venice (today Galleria dell'Accademia), this is among the earliest appreciations of woodcarving work that have come down to us. Nevertheless we are dealing here with a genre and with an outstanding example with which the work of the cabinetmaker Etienne Louis Infroit cannot be compared. The special field of the latter was just the picture frame, which as achievement became worthy of mention in a sphere of art only recently arrived at independence. Here only the virtuosity of the execution counted, whereas before it was usually not the maker who was named, but only the coordinating entrepreneur, who had usually delegated to others the execution of individual parts. This kind of documentary record was the custom with choir stalls, pulpits and altars, just as with comprehensive decorative plans for rooms.

In the larger workshops it had long been customary for various specialists to collaborate in frame making. Since the Middle Ages carving work and the making of moldings were as a rule in other hands than the mounting and gilding. Thus in 1507 Dürer wrote to Jacob Heller that he had "disengaged" the panel from the joiner and then had turned it over to a "preparer" or "finishing artist" who had primed and "colored" it and wished to gild it in the following week. Further rationalization can be seen in the picture shown in Fig. 2. Strips and moldings were made separately by the length, while chalk priming, engraved designs and mountings were obtained from specialists. Finally from the early 19th century onward the preparation of plastic ornamentation was separated from the woodwork. Through the use of papier mâché, gilding compound and plaster of Paris, cheaper reproduction of the negative forms now cut in wooden molds became possible.

From the contracts that have come down to us one can determine the value of the craftsmanship from the costs for some frames. For the high altar of Santissima Annunciata in Florence the painter Filippino Lippi received — according to Vasari — 200 gold scudi. The frame maker Baccio d'Agnolo, however, received 250 gold scudi and a further 200 were spent for the gilding. Similarly high were the prices for frames paid to the sculptor Giulano da San Gallo. For the frame of a Botticelli picture ("Madonna with Child and Two Saints," painted in 1485 for the Bardi Chapel in S. Spirito in Florence and now in the Dahlem Gallery in Berlin) he received 24 gold florins (gold gulden), 8 soldi and 5 danari, which presumably also included the preparation of the panel for the picture. The painter Boticelli obtained 75 florins and 15 soldi, of which 2 florins were intended for the ultramarine blue and 38 florins for the gold and the gilding of the frame. How far the frame around the London picture of the Botticelli workshop can be brought into connection with San Gallo is for the present an open question (Ill. 61).

Later contracts relate to the execution of frames in magnificent style, which were then to be produced not just by some craftsman or other but by a sculptor. An example is the sumptuous frame that Thomas Schwanthaler was commissioned in 1702 to carve, to mount and to gild for 30 gulden on the order of the Reichersberg Foundation. Such information is on the whole very rare — and still rarer are the cases in which the works named have survived. As a rule the frames fell victim to changes in taste or else have survived thanks only to those ruthless adaptations. The rare case of a painting, and moreover a valuable one, being adapted to a frame (by shortening the format) is represented by the manneristic frame in the magnificent style shown (Ill. 105).

In addition to such knowledge handed down directly, an important source of information is the depiction of frames on pictures, drawings and engravings. Since the 15th century, churches and the inside rooms of houses had been portrayed as the settings of many scenes, even though in idealized form. To them we owe our knowledge of the earliest forms of panel paintings mounted independently on the wall (as, for example, in Carpaccio's representation of the bedchamber of Saint Ursula, painted between 1490 and 1500 and in the contemporaneous picture of the Miracle of the cross by Mansueti, both now in Venice in the Galleria dell'Accademia). Later, after the end of the 16th century, there arose gallery pictures and depictions of small and large cabinets of art objects and curios, on which pictures were faithfully portrayed with their appropriate frames. Thus from the Flemish paintings of interiors it can be proved, for example, that the "Battle of the Amazons" by Rubens (now in the Alte Pinakothek in Munich) first carried a relatively wide strip frame, then a narrower one, long before it received the magnificent gilded frame that it still carries today.

The class of paintings of interiors that came into being in the 17th century provides additional knowledge about styles of furnishing and therewith also of frames. Some interesting details can be taken from contemporaneous engravings, as, for example, the observation in the case of Abraham Bosse of the hanging of pictures over tapestry (in numerous engravings, see Fig. 7). This kind of documentary evidence reaches all the way from engravings showing

Fig. 2. Frame-Gilder's Studio from Diderot and d'Alembert's *Encyclopaedie,* Paris 1751-65.

a. View of the Studio

1. Artisan applying red under-coating
2. Artisan cutting ornamentation
3. Artisan gilding the easel
4. Artisan polishing
5. Artisan applying chalk base
6. Artisan embossing

The sequence of steps is 5-2-1-3-4-6. The equipment is the traditional, still largely in use today. It is interesting that as early as the time of Louis XVI carved moldings, measuring approximately two meters in length, were prepared in advance. Presumably the same procedure was followed for simple profile moldings.

b. The Tools

1. Roller for crushing chalk
2. Tray for crushing chalk
3. Hollow chisel for cutting ornamentation
4. Hollow chisel of different shape
5. Curved and pointed chisels
6. Agate polishing tool
7. Knife for cutting gold leaf
8. Palette with brush
9. Pumice stone to smoothen surfaces
10. Sponge
11. Square rod
12. Easel
13. Cushion, covered with leather, for cutting gold foil
14. Pointed knife for cutting foil
15. Brush for spreading sand for stipple effect
16. Grounding brush
17. Small grounding brush
18. Small brush for applying red undercoating
19. Large brush for applying red undercoating
20. Workbench for an assistant
21. Vat for preparing the chalk mixture

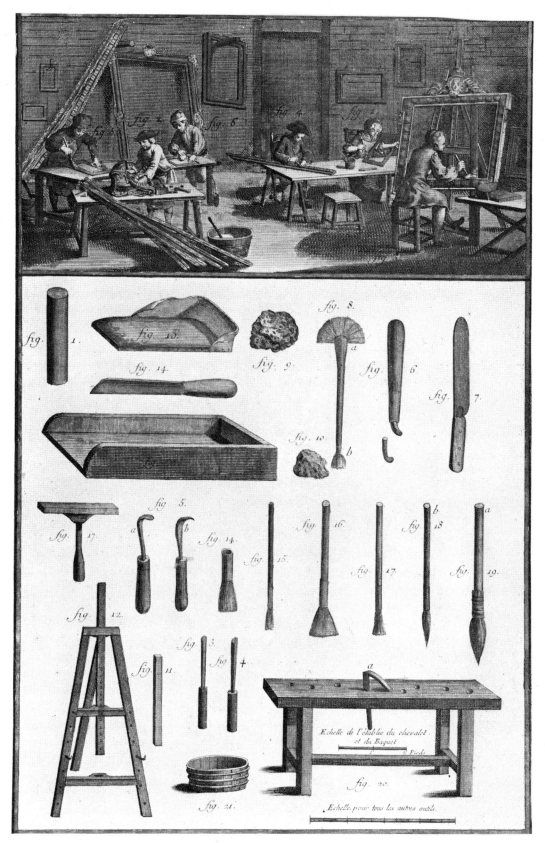

Fig. 3. Emanuel de Witte (1617-92). Detail of a frame with curtain for a family portrait, 1678. *Munich, Bayerische Gemäldesammlungen.*

examples of furnishing (Fig. 23) up to the first photographs of the exhibition walls of the Realists and Impressionists.

For a general view the sources named are certainly full of gaps. Only an extremely small number of the historically authenticated and recorded frames can be traced today. Even in the case of works of art that have remained in place—in churches, palaces and manor houses —the original framing has seldom been preserved. One can prove the originals only by employing all possible means of checking. First of all the technique of the craftsmanship must be taken into consideration, then the type of wood must be examined, the style of the joinery work, the priming coats of picture and frame. It is rare for the correlation between picture and frame to be recognizable so simply with the naked eye as in the picture from the Upper Rhine of the Annunciation (Ill. 39), in which the cracks in the wood go uniformly through picture and frame, showing that both are out of one piece, that is to say, not nailed together but carved out. Procuring exhaustive information on the origin, type and age of a frame these days has to include investigation of the structure of the wood and the chronology of the tree just as much as X-ray, infrared and infrared reflectograph exposures. This has been

performed for only a few pieces. The amount of work required—from the removal of some firmly gilded frames up to and including taking the frames partly to pieces—is also worthwhile only when clear information can be obtained on a large number of related questions.

For the majority of the frames that have come down to us the classification according to style groups and art landscapes is of prime importance. The types that can be definitely dated and localized can give indications in this respect. Knowledge of species of wood and some characteristic constructional features help in narrowing the estimate of place and date, likewise knowledge of the ornamentation—from the patterns of carving as well as their variation in all genres of handicrafts. Few museums of the world have up to now made an inventory of their frames. The Metropolitan Museum of Art, New York, must be mentioned as a praiseworthy exception, and possibly the Museum of Fine Arts in Boston will shortly do the same. The National Gallery in London has started with an inventorial card index and other museums are similarly collecting historical material on individual frames in their possession. Since the initiative taken by Wilhelm von Bode, the original framings of the pictures and reliefs exhibited are noted in the Berlin catalog. During

Fig. 4. "Kunstkammer" of a doll's house with miniature pictures and frames. Late 17th century. *Utrecht, Centraal Museum.*

recent times the Ashmolean Museum in Oxford has been continuously dealing in its bulletins with questions of gallery framing and the corresponding new acquisitions. A selection from the fund of Italian frames of the Alte Pinakothek in Munich was the subject of a small exhibition and of a catalog that also reported on investigations into wood structure. The photographs of moldings and mountings collected by the Österreichisches Bundesdenkmalamt (Federal Austrian Bureau for the Preservation of Historical Memorials) should furnish an important contribution to our knowledge of the framing of altarpieces. For a long time they have been making full-sized partial copies of woodwork joints and mountings of all authenticated old frames or restored workshop pieces.

A problem of no less importance has up to now scarcely been dealt with: that of the differing functions of contemporaneous frames. The museum visitor of today expects an expensive frame around an expensive picture, a tabernacle frame, for example, for Leonardo da Vinci's "Ginevra da Benci," and a quiet, unobtrusive frame around a contemporaneous but anonymous picture of the Virgin Mary. Or he visualizes a Rembrandt portrait rather splenddidly framed and one of the inevitable portraits

of a ruling prince framed with more restraint. Yet it was absolutely certain that the ecclesiastical devotional pictures — most magnificent at the places of pilgrimage (Ill. 329) — and the imposing courtly representations were the ones that received the most brilliant "robes" in the form of their frames. In former times the function of the painting regulated the framing more than did the rank of the artist, the estimation of whom had in any case changed many times. To realize this one needs only to compare the various original Dürer frames: that of the All Saints picture (Ill. 64); that of the "Four Apostles" (Ill. 30) intended for a secular room; and the narrow frame, unfortunately covered over, of the portrait of Hieronymus Holzschuher (Ill. 440). In spite of the continual secularization of a form that in earlier times was purely ecclesiastical and in spite of the various branches of art becoming increasingly bourgeois since the 17th century, these gradations in significance are recognizable on the frame right up to the Age of Enlightenment.

Some clues to the former functions of picture and frame remain in details still visible today. Holes and recesses for hinges have been preserved on some late Gothic frames, thus showing that they were portions of diptychs or triptychs (Ill 35, 41); sometimes this original

Fig. 5. Jean Colombe (?-1529). "Boethius in the Library of His Monastery." Title miniature in *Consolation de la philosophie de Boèce,* dated 1476. This is the earliest example of a hanging picture. *London, British Library.*

Fig. 6. Wall of the gallery in Melk Convent, Austria. One of the rare surviving examples of a Baroque gallery. The frames are uniformly executed in an early classicizing manner.

connection itself has also been preserved (Ill. 29, 51, 52). Direct evidence (Ill. 41) and indirect (Fig. 3) can been seen from the former rods and cord-eyes. These served for fixing a curtain that could be drawn closed to protect the picture — or also to conceal it as a specially valuable object. Sliding covers had the same purpose. Old frames, up to and including those of the early 18th century, have many times been preserved that show a slit on the outside edge of one of the border rails. The sliding cover was inserted into this slit at the side or from above in front of the surface of the picture, and was held by suitable guide grooves on the inside edge of the frame. Unfortunately not one single frame has come down to us together with its cover. The sole "cover" authenticated by tradition is preserved today divided into two parts, namely on Albrecht Dürer's portrait of Oswolt Krel (Munich, Alte Pinakothek), the composition of which has been altered in the 20th century to a triptych form. As can be recognized in an engraving by Abraham Bosse (A. Blum, Bosse, 1924, Plates 7, 8), in the 17th century there still existed the standing or lean-to style of picture, which traditionally at one time probably comprised the larger number of older portrait paintings as well as the small devotional pictures, which were brought out of storage, folded out or pushed open only for some definite purpose. Where the old picture panels have been preserved undivided they frequently show painted backs with an immaculate surface, which would have been hardly possible if they had been hanging for a long time against a wall, and still less against rough and damp masonry. For particular frames specific constructional requirements thereby went together with the peculiar usage for which the pictures were intended: memorial plaques, votive pictures, epitaphs — these are very closely related to those objects that are used for meditation and for prayer.

As the examples mentioned indicate, within short periods of time there were many different functions for frames themselves. Yet even the traditional functions recognizable as existing side by side were as a whole subjected to a thoroughgoing historical change that revised all their meanings. The historical survey does indeed proceed from the concept that a basic material form — the frame — became for a limited space of time the vehicle of significant meanings. On the other hand certain curvatures in its cross section, its outline, its appearance as brought about by coloring and ornamentation show far-reaching changes. These are not random or arbitrary changes. They are rather the traces left by a history that increasingly differentiated the actual from the esthetic, the reality of knowledge from the reality of mind; and the insight into the picture therewith lost its power of suggestion and the gold of the frame forfeited its quality of magic.

The following survey describes the reinterpretation and the reshaping from time to time of the significance of "frame" as it has come down through the centuries. To keep this book within bounds only the independent *mobile* frames have been considered. Cassettes, framings of ceiling pictures and inclosures of inset wall paintings have had to be omitted.

Fig. 7. Abraham Bosse (1602-76). Detail from a sheet of the series of "The Wise and Foolish Virgins," 1635, exemplifying the placement of pictures on wall hangings.

Historical Survey

Very Early Forms of Picture Framing

The forms of frame décor of the later Occidental art have to a large extent been determined by the forms of décor of Greco-Roman antiquity. Richly varied ornaments in great diversity are found on portal surrounds and door panels, window jambs and the capitals of columns. Celtic, Germanic and Oriental elements are in late classical and early medieval art mixed with the patterns of classical décor found in ancient buildings. The ornamentation on ecclesiastical buildings and the framings of the small and large pieces of sculpture that have survived furnish information on the assimilation and reinterpretation of their traditional forms.

The question whether in classical times or in the early Middle Ages there were "frames" in our sense of the word cannot be answered. Certainly there were few pictures serving as movable furnishings for any and every private room. But in stately secular rooms there were already areas painted with illusionistic pictures, which were surrounded with ornamental bands and painted friezes; this is proved by the late classical wall painting. It is tempting to conclude from such areas of wall decoration, and also from the early medieval miniatures in their painted framings, that there were contemporaneous panel pictures and fully sculptured frames. A conclusion of this kind is especially suggested by the somewhat overstrained three-dimensional illusionism of an early medieval painting (Ill. 5), in which the footrest of the evangelist portrayed appears to project over the zone of the frame, which has been executed

to suggest a molded form. Werner Ehlich cites the "concave molded frame with acanthus-leaf ornament, silvered and gilded" as additional evidence of antique framing. The same author has also collected together the other arguments that speak in favor of pictures set up free on bronze stands and fixed on walls. Portable pictures of the emperor on wooden panels or stone slabs, portraits of ancestors and painted portraits of important persons and their families, representations of battles and pictures of gods are authenticated by literary sources, and we also know that they were set up and hung in public places (thermal baths, meeting halls, temples). But the character of these pictures — in some cases consecrated — is difficult to reconstruct. Ehlich's reconstructions of the pictures on folding panels testify that the corresponding frames show unaccustomed combinations with decorative borders for the practical purpose of fastening, as also in the descriptions of the stucco borders around mummy portraits (Ill. 2).

Both the classical and early medieval reliefs and miniatures teach us that there were always two basic types of pictorial representation that determined the form of the frame. The upright picture, the frame of which acted as the canopy of a spatial figure, existed side by side with the recumbent picture as a world in itself, the framing of which is directed uniformly from the inside to the outside (Ill. 6, 7). This contrast continued right up to the "art nouveau" of the 20th century in varying combinations in the types of frame chosen.

It is difficult to determine the significance of the architectonic and plant-form elements that were used at various times in the zone of the frame. The detail of the framing of a book cover (the Codex Aureus of St. Emmeram, Ill. 8) here serves as evidence that acanthus leaves, palmettes and strings of pearls can, according to the medieval interpretation, be signs of salvation and the coming dominion of Christ (in the temple of the second Jerusalem). The plants signified, as did the material of gold and of precious stones, carriers of magic. Some remains of this meaning still cling to the gold mountings of the Baroque period, which were probably conceived as being incomparably valuable and as having in their appearance the highest symbolic quality.

Architectonic Framing

The medieval tabular antependia (in front of the altar table) and the picture panels set up on the altar since the 13th century were at the latest parts of the church equipment. They fitted into the group of tasks required for a presentation of "church" as a whole, as it was conceived in those times; that is to say, of a theologically and liturgically organized representation. The framing of the surfaces of pictures was thereby a demarcation from wall areas and walls of a room. The simple framing, consisting only of flat and beveled pieces, corresponds to the theoretical linkage of "pictures." The corresponding surrounds are either projecting edges, left standing, of the wooden panels which had been recessed to make the surface of the picture (consequently original parts thereof), or they were applied to the wooden panels from the front.

According to the requirements of statics from time to time, some of these frames overlap the surface of the picture at the sides. In principle they fulfill the same function as other spatial demarcations, such as the fitting of arches and of door and window jambs. Yet this form of frame (Ill. 9) that had already arisen in the 13th century shows representative tendencies beyond mere spatial demarcation. The outline of the frame took on façade, gable and portal forms and therewith typical characteristics of the form of the church building. Even though painted picture surfaces were originally only parts of an overall esthetic concept, that is, of an architectural concept, nevertheless in the structure of the altar they received independence in several respects. Following the same development the altar frame, a little later,

was sculpturally articulated. In form and moldings it took over structural elements of architecture and in its substance became architectonic itself and similar to a building.

This kind of transfer of outward forms can be observed right through medieval art (Ill. 13), and explains the relationships among the forms of buildings, furniture and implements that jump over differences of material and format. This transfer was not, however, the result of arbitrary fancy. The growth, the fashioning, and the refinement of the form of the altar did not proceed from some caprice of decoration nor did these clearly indicate an inclusion in an aimless differentiation of the forms of representation, but arose from the transfer of artistic activities to the liturgical field, to specific, easily understandable manifestations of the religious idea. The richly detailed altar forms of the 14th, 15th and early 16th centuries evolved into many elements, having finally taken over in their plan something of the pretensions of the erstwhile church building; in their connection to portal and façade forms (in Italy) and to nave and façade details (in France and Germany) they show a "church within a church." What at one time was striven after in the embellishment of the church building with a large number of figures appears here brought close together in a systematic sequence of pictures of the Redemption. The frames of the big triptychs, polyptychs and folding altars form architectonic structures connected in their type to "church," "temple" and "shrine." The representative function of these structures and the function of demarcating the areas of the individual pictures overlap and can be separated from each other to some extent only in Dutch and German art. The contrast in the conceptions of art makes the difference in development comprehensible. The arrangement of multipartite sequences of pictures of saints and of pictorial scenes remains in Italy an optical problem: picture areas of varying formats clash with each other and are placed in a flat overall form. Even in the altars provided with rich structures there exists a close relationship to the formats of the individual pictures. Expressed as a formula, the Italian altar in its substance has always remained a "picture panel," which by means of its form makes particularly evident from time to time the close relation to "church," to "dispensation" (for this see the representation of nature-healing symbolized by the medicinal plants in the windows of the frame superstructure of Gentile da Fabriano's

Fig. 8. Fra Filippo Lippi (1406-69). Sketch for an altarpiece triptych and its frame, 1457. *Florence, Archivio di Stato.*

altar, Ill. 15). The development from the 15th to the 16th century can be described as the carrying through and rendering uniform of a symbology of pictorial projection instead of spatial patterns. In this the guiding purpose remained the bringing of the metaphysical order into a form perceptible through the senses, a transition which was, however, bound up with the development of the language of art.

As can be repeatedly substantiated since the writings of Thomas Aquinas (1224-1274), works of art in Italy were not regarded as literal representations, but as creations that could present an idealistic reality only through the degree of their perfection, and this strengthened the tendency towards making the altars as a whole uniform, and likewise the decorative and theatrical intensification of dominant motifs. This is illustrated by the altar of Gentile da Fabriano, which stands at the end of the development of multipartite altar housings and at the beginning of a new pictorial unity (Ill. 15). The broken-out form of frame—also an intermediate stage—as a structural form becomes finally neglected. A splendid panorama-like pictorial scene is unfolded, going right through the existing arrangement of panels. The significance of the crowning gables is changed into that of a rich decoration. The remaining tectonic elements in the form of the lateral edges of the frame are moved as flanks forward of the plane of the picture—as octagonal shafts for a construction that spatially is no longer carried through. The architectural forms have thereby become decorative members released from their former functional significance. The

portrayals on the gable areas and in the base of the predella do indeed still combine into an integrating order, but this completion of the program is a decorative accessory, subordinate to the mise-en-scène of the central stage. The importance of the outline (contrasted, for example, with Ill. 17 as a form tied to tradition) has become just as faded as the connecting internal structure (examples of triptychs and polyptychs of the big altars are not recorded in the illustrations; for this compare the illustrations in the works of Elfried Bock and Monika Cämmerer-George). From this it can be inferred that the intention of using tectonic and static formulae for the symbolization of a higher order was given up. These handed-down ciphers were superseded in favor of a new-style, nature-oriented, illusionistic art, in which the forms of order were those of perceptual perspectives and of scenic staging.

Anticipations of a pictorial theatrical stage consistently adapted to the visual order can already be found in the paintings of Giotto (1266-1337); corresponding innovations in the framing can be seen from the same master. The framing around Giotto's "Ognissanti Madonna" (Florence, Uffizi) shows for the first time something like a "pure" picture frame. The preliminary stages of this were the 13th century frames provided with moldings (as with Guida da Siena, Cimabue and Duccio), furthest developed in Duccio's "Madonna Rucellai" (1275, Florence, Uffizi, detail in Ill. 12).

Already with Duccio the frame bevel has become a gradation of moldings which indicate an individual architectonic character. Certainly the flat, ribbon-like treatment of the surrounding frame panel leads the imagination back to the dividing strips of the wall areas. The insertion of the thirty frame medallions in association with the edicle form points in the direction of the multipartite, flat altarpiece systems, which came into being a little later.

In contrast to this Giotto's frame presents itself from every angle as molded frame. The frame panel forming the boundary has shrunk to a narrow outside edge. The molding sequence leaves out a narrow intermediate path, which is ornamented in a manner similar to the previous frame panels. This path is converted into a concave molding between the rising, strongly convex moldings on each side. Out of the elements of architectonic transition and intermediate structure, concave channel and molding, an original form has emerged. Subse-

Fig. 9. Altura Montovano (?). Design for an altarpiece including its frame, c.1520/30. *Oxford, Christ Church College.*

Fig. 10. Anonymous Italian artist of the early 17th century. Sketch of a wall or ceiling decoration of a gallery frame. *London, Victoria and Albert Museum.*

quently this form came clearly into prominence everywhere where independent pictorial works, unified portrayals of an artistic concept complete in itself, were present. In the case of the altarpieces the range of subjects represented became extended, as stated, which means that correlations of ideas worth representing and capable of being experienced were possible only by embedding them in the structure of theological notions. The small picture panels, however, as clearly demarcated pictorial units, took the place of the big altarpieces in the field of private devotions.

Besides the forms with architectural silhouette (Ill. 17) a large number of rectangular formats have survived from the 14th and early 15th centuries with molded frames, which have at times rather the character of a casing rising outwards and at times that of a panel set with swelling rolls. The manner in which individual pictorial areas have become independent is shown in the quatrefoil-shaped frame moldings, repeated in many rows, to be found in the bronze doors of the Florentine baptistry (Ill. 10). They in their turn are again inclosed in rectangular areas, which are likewise framed with moldings. Here it is probably more a matter of bordering the door surface put into the foreground, from which surface the portrayals are seen as through windows. The repetition of this motif in the 26 panels of the former cabinet of holy relics in the sacristy of Santa Croce in Florence shows an unusual pictorial concept

(which was presumably tied to the notion of transportation, that is, to the intermediary role assigned to the relics and their receptacle.)

The secular frames, which no longer appeared as bound to ecclesiastical functions, were preceded in Italy by an intermediary form of ecclesiastical altarpiece framing. The change in the pictures that brought about this development consisted in the repression of everything transcendental, of all symbolism that represented nothing perceptible through the senses, in favor of an attempt at coming to terms with visible nature and its fundamental laws. The beauty of the proportions and the reciprocal harmony of the forms provided, as idealized patterns, indications of a supernatural quality. Although at the start remaining within the traditional religious subjects, nevertheless the configurations employed for symbolic purposes were concentrated upon quite general concepts and laws of form. The artistically purest, most primordial shapes expressed this ideal: the return to the classical Graeco-Roman canons of form signified the use of the structures of temple façades for church façades as also for altarpiece frames. The earliest example of a homogeneous retable frame that can be regarded as Renaissance architecture is fixed around Fra Angelico's Pala of the "Annunciation" of 1431-1434 (in Cortona, Museo Diocesano). The surface-decorated wood is used for a construction of pure architectural forms.

Fig. 11. William Kent (1685-1748). Sketch of a chimney piece with framed picture, which was to be executed in 1733. *London, Victoria and Albert Museum.*

Fig. 12. Abraham Drentwett (1647-1729). Engraved designs of frames for paintings or mirrors.

Since then the architectonic form of housing — with and without gable — is found framing pictures of all formats. One encounters them on big altarpieces, where they are termed "edicule." The smaller formats of this type, derived from tabernacle forms of the same design, are called "tabernacle frames." With these small frames in particular (Ill. 54-57) the portion immediately surrounding the picture is strongly emphasized — up to the forms around 1500, in which this has become the flat, or plate, frame.

A newly-created type of frame, the "Tondo," connects similarly ornamented decorative surfaces, as encountered on the horizontal and vertical flat borders of the tabernacle frames. Often set off with flat moldings or decorative staves on the inside and outside edges, the dominant frame molding consists of a garland of leaves going all around, or of an ornamental fillet (Ill. 59-62). This circular form probably goes back to the similarly inclosed Madonna relievos of Luca ·della Robbia (1399-1482).

Paintings with religious themes still predominate in the second half of the 15th century; in artistic significance these represent in any case the most important commissions, and the magnificent frames must have been intended for them. The products later designated as merely "handicraft" work were, especially in the furnishing of rooms as in churches and chapels, part of the interior decoration and contribute to the ornamentation. The frames of the big altarpieces were not only priced just as highly as the pictures inserted into them, but were often ordered and made long before the pictures that were to be painted. Thus the frame cited of Baccio d'Agnolo was already commissioned in 1500, whereas the order to the painter Filippino was placed in 1503. Similarly, regarding the sequence of frame and picture, the information has come down to us that the frame by the woodcarver Giacomo del Maino had first to be completed before Leonardo da Vinci could take up the work on his rock-grotto Madonna — and also on the painting and gilding of the frame.

Late Gothic Frames in Germany and the Netherlands

In contrast to the visual unity of the altarpiece in Italy, there exist in the multipartite German and Dutch altarpieces very few points of correspondence between the structure as a whole and the framings of the individual pictures. The altar case, presumably developed out of the tradition of the cabinets of holy relics, is into the 16th century a cabinet of considerable depth, both of the center portion and also of the stand and the superstructure (upper works). The altar case frequently contains combinations of various genres of representation: sculptures, mezzo-relievos and paintings and, moreover, above or below the main zone of portrayal, also vessels with holy relics (Ill. 18 shows an early example). The contents are displayed only after opening out the panels. The overreaching spiritual framework of "dispensation" or "church" is made visible only in the upper sections of the panel surfaces (Ill. 13, 19), later in the three-dimensional figurate headpiece on the altar cabinet. Nevertheless, a continuous form such as can be found in the Italian folding altarpieces placed as a unifying element over the individual pictures (Ill. 18 shows this in small format) is not found here.

With Jan van Eyck (active 1422-1441) all that remains is merely a kind of indication of type in the partly flat frame. The feature in common is the molding on the inside edge and the surface finish in imitation of stone or marble (Ill. 33, 34). A few panels in small format have on the lower edge the "watershed," copied from the sloping surface at the base of church windows for allowing water to run off. The portal and canopy framing, defining the impression the picture is to make, is taken into the illusionistic scheme of many pictures, as shown in an old-fashioned variant in a small triptych (Ill. 29), which an anonymous artist created shortly before the works of van Eyck.

For the Netherlands and Germany the frame types newly formulated by van Eyck continued to set the style until the end of the century. Only the decoration of the flat frame members varied. The framing having a semicircular upper portion with a flat frame set off inside and outside by moldings or edges (Ill. 67, 68) is also among the types going back to the workshop of van Eyck. Simplified stylizations of the frame form, taken from the architecture of doors and windows, are also exemplified by the subdividing ribs or bars observed later, as they are laid lattice-like on the hollow molding — "fluting" — in the picture from Michael Pacher's altarpiece of St. Wolfgang (Ill. 28) or on the frame of Albrecht Dürer's "Four Apostles" (Ill. 30).

To the visible evidences of the altar unit, which can otherwise be observed only from time to time by turning the wings of the altarpiece, there belong motifs that recur in the ornamentation of the front of many frames: the "Jesse Root," the "Rosebush," the "Grapevine" (Ill. 28, 29, 32). These connecting motifs, representing the genealogy of Christ or his power of salvation, penetrate as carved nature-motifs into the architectonic structure of the altarpieces. They reach from the base right up into

the headpiece and wind themselves along the body of the altarpiece (Ill. 31).

Secular Frames

The late Middle Ages had increasingly illustrated the religious subjects of their pictures with worldly motifs and in forms of observation accessible to everyone. Whether the ideal was sought in the perfection of artistic form — of the proportions, lines and surface effects — as in Italy, or in the convincing illusion of elements of supernatural events, as in the North, artistic presentation had become the means of shaping forth a higher nature. The new artistic message of the pictures had acquired indications of meaning that could be interpreted not merely as theological and religious in the narrow sense but could equally point to a special historical, moral and scientific characteristic. In the 16th century, landscapes became independent allegories of the cosmic cycle of day and night, of the occurrence and evanescence of the seasons; still-life pictures showed the ephemeral connections of the four elements, ideal figures bringing human concepts into the foreground. The depiction of a religious motif was a special case only of the artistic in general. The Italian art of the frame caused richly decorated flat frames, with diminishing headpieces and bases, to evolve out of the edicle and tabernacle frames (Ill. 53-57). Here also the use for secular purposes of pictures in flat and molded frames still continued in the 15th century. The intense feeling in the enframing, that in any case came to the fore only in the general humanistic sense, had been successfully applied to the self-assured secular art, admittedly at all times moderated in accordance with the degree of objectivity of the motif of the picture.

· Among the earliest examples of panels from a winged altarpiece are the Worms panels (Ill. 19, 20) dated around 1260, which are formed with the typical difference between the outer and inner sides. This is particularly true of the frame surfaces. On the outside, these slightly raised border zones are articulated by means of leaf and loop motifs placed separately, not flowing around like a ribbon. In contrast to this pattern, probably the expression of nature-mystic formulae, the inside directly presents the material luster of gold, of magic significance. Stone and cross-stone patterns illustrate the gem-like and metallic qualities. The decorative

Fig. 13.   Jean Lepautre (1618-82). Engraved design of a picture frame.

bordered edging of the picture panels has thereby the function of providing a kind of material delimitation of the pictorial domain. The blossom, star and leaf motifs stamped onto other frames (Ill. 24, 26, 27, 29, 32) point in the same direction, likewise the suggestions of inlaid precious stones and relics (Ill. 24, 25).

Already in the Worms panels a shallow grooved molding is laid between the frame and the surface of the picture. The sense of this allusion is that the frame is to be understood "before" the picture. North of the Alps also a progressive "architectonization" occurs right into the 15th century, which, however, has nothing to do with the structural casing of the frame as a whole, but with the enhanced illusion within each individual picture of looking through at a vista. For this the frame, in a quite matter-of-fact way, both limits the picture and leads the eye into it. Starting from the metaphysical character of the ecclesiastical world of pictures, a design was used obviously analogous to the outside structure of the late Gothic churches. Their portals and windows afforded views into a room in which the world of salvation, of Paradise, became present, in accordance with the belief in the church as the site of the coming Second Jerusalem. To render the illusion of these views into the higher world compelling,

the room in which they are housed must be unmistakably differentiated from the reality of the worldly setting. Accordingly, in northern Europe from the beginning of the new-style panel pictures onward the forms and properties of the material of church window and church portal were transferred onto the form of the individual frame, which, worked out as a door or window wall, permitted only a constricted view. The examples range from the framing of sculptured figures (Ill. 13) to the similarly constricted directing of the eye to paintings. The masterpiece of this transference, not illustrated here, is the "Bargello Diptych" (French, around 1390, Florence, Museo Nazionale, illustrated in the works of Stange/Cremer and Heydenryk).

With the beginning of the 15th century, interest lapsed in the transferential structure of this style of frame directed inward to the picture. The zone of the frame stepped back into a subsidiary function in comparison to the message of the picture. The manner of looking at and of assessing the value of a picture that had in the meantime come to the fore seems in the Netherlands and in Germany to have rendered superfluous the symbolic preparation of the observer by means of the frame. Only one example of French art preserved in small format ("Mary and Child" by an unknown master, between 1400 and 1430, in a frame of the same wood, New York, Frick Collection, illustrated in the book by Heydenryk) suggests that further examples have existed there of a style of framing in which comprehensible traditional decorative elements are combined with a transitional form toward the molded frame.

In the Netherlands also the portraits that were separated out from the religious pictures of founder and worshipper represented an intermediate stage toward secular subject-matter. The portrayal, at the beginning still semi-religious, "sub specie aeternitas" (which treats portraits like memorial stones—makes them into votive and devotional pictures), takes over for this reason not only motifs of architectonic painting (Ill. 33, 38, 47), but also the outline forms of altarpieces or memorial stones (Ill. 50-52) and the arrangement in diptychs and triptychs. Nevertheless, there are striking ambiguities in the symbolical marking of the material of the frames: thus in the case of van Eyck's portrait of his wife the back is also marbleized, and too, the inscriptions in the case of another portrait by van Eyck and of one by Hans Memling (Ill. 38) are emphasized as though cut in with a chisel. Monika

Fig. 14. Rembrandt van Rijn (1606-69). Design of the frame for the painting "The Sermon of John the Baptist." Pen and brush; c.1655. *Paris, Musée du Louvre.*

Cämmerer-George has understood these and other features observed as indicating that the stone frame is here not taken from church architecture but represents a flat tombstone.

A distinction was made right into the Baroque period, according to the claim to importance of the class of picture, between the elegant types of frame, where edicle frames continued to exist on altars, and the flat frames of modest elaboration for secular pictures (as can be seen on most of the old gallery pictures). An appropriately sumptuous frame was, above the picture mounting, an elevated supplement to the subject portrayed. In the case of Dürer's All Saints picture the frame, which was executed according to his draft design (Ill. 64), contains a depiction of the Last Judgment. This takes precedence thematically over the "Adoration of the Trinity," which is portrayed in the painting. The picture itself is fastened onto a carrier frame, which had to be laid into the architectonic frame. In contrast to this, the frame of the "Four Apostles" itself forms the carrier frame for the wooden boards of the painting, which for this reason are – exceptionally – arranged transversely to the format of the picture; in this way they are best secured. The late Renaissance and the early Baroque then put an

end to the canon of the edicle framing for religious portrayals in small format.

Painted Frames

A charming tradition, reminiscent of the antique, remained preserved from the time of polyptych framing until the Romantic period: that of the painted frames. Just as the architectonic frame casing had to house supplementary portrayals and symbolic allusions, which completed the totality of the temple of ecclesiastical salvation, so the smaller devotional presentations, especially during the Counter-Reformation, took this up again. In Spain as in Flanders the framing of religious pictures with mystical emblems was revived (Ill. 71) from the late 16th century onward. A tradition leading into the painted frame comes moreover from the picture tabernacle, from the form, prevalent since the late Middle Ages, of the insertion of established traditional pictures of miracle-working saints into the surfaces of larger pictures. During the Baroque period some individual orders also caused specialists to paint garlands of flowers on wide frames, into which relatively small devotional pictures were then

33

Fig. 15. Gabriel Metsu (1629-67). Details of Dutch picture and mirror frames from "Lady Reading a Letter and Her Maid," c.1665/70. *Ireland, Beit Collection.*

inserted (the picture gallery of the Bode-Museum in East Berlin has a work of this kind by the still-life painter Jan Davidsz de Heem).

Italian Regional Frames from the Quattrocento to the late Baroque

Some individual regional paintings can in the various historical periods show definite focal points of artistic achievement. Specially intensive ornamental animation of even the simple flat and molded frames quite generally characterizes Italian art in the 15th and 16th centuries. Ane yet during this period Italy included regions artistically very independent, among which Siena, Florence and Venice stand in the forefront in the art of the frame. In the 16th century Bologna, in addition, became prominent.

A pronounced linearity, a lack of plasticity, can be observed in the Sienese art of the frame. The shallow moldings partition off compartment-like areas, which are filled with varying decoration, chiefly of entwined patterns. Molded bars and decorative embellishment, geometric and well-balanced, emphasize an overall two-dimensional form. The body of the frame, however, stands out only slightly from

the surface of the picture or of the wall. Not only do the examples in illustrations 77-79 show this tendency, but also the "Tondo" in illustration 62.

In contrast to this the Florentine art of the frame shows a more decided working out of the basic form and of three-dimensional dynamics. Moldings stress the inside and outside edges in relation to the frame surface. The ornamentation—whether on sumptuous (Ill. 81) or on plain frames (Ill. 80)—remains a restrained inner structure within a dominant general form.

In the Venetian frames this homogeneous inclusive impression is neglected. There the tabernacle and edicle forms of the 14th and 15th century frames do not possess the static clarity and figurative consistency found in the Florentine region (Elfried Bock has worked this out in detail; see also illustrations 53-57). Already in the altarpiece framings of the 14th and 15th centuries a very diversified decoration captures the attention. So far as an all-inclusive characterization of this is possible, it can be said that the Venetian frames consist more than anywhere else of structures composed of elements with delicate and precious ornamentation which, however, are not allocated to any well-marked comprehensive form. A magnificent example like the frame around Bellini's

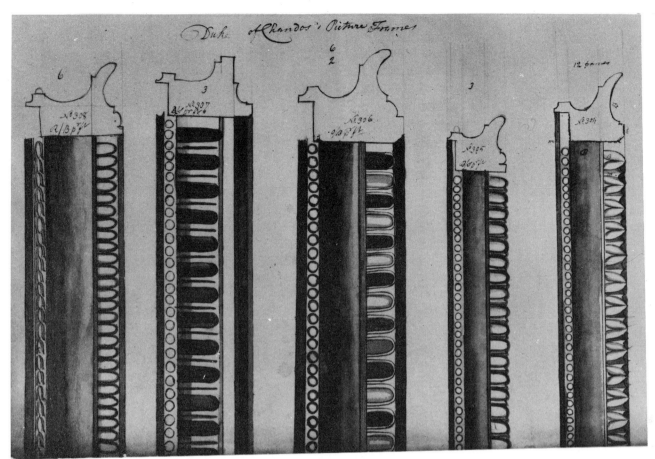

Fig. 16. John Linnell (?-1796). Designs for frame profiles and ornamentation for paintings in the collection of the Duke of Chandos. From the Linnell Album, c.1778. *London, Victoria and Albert Museum.*

altarpiece in the Frari church in Venice (Ill. 63) demonstrates this predominance of two-dimensional decoration. Although this is arranged as an edicle, all important structural ele-ments are omitted; there are no massive plinths and heavy beams, no supporting columns and flush capitals. Where such motifs occur they act only as foils to a kind of mezzo-relievo decoration. This frame, made in 1488 by Jacopo da Faenza, reproduces a motif several times repeated. The frame has neither a dominating structure linking together the area to be comtemplated, nor its own independent architectonic standard of form; it is rather the projecting forward edge of the illusionistic theatrical architecture of the picture.

The frames in medium and small format with — at one time gilded — pastiglia decoration are in their optical impression dominated by the rhythm of the ornamental ribbon-like bands that over a wide surface overlay the central path, mostly convex, of the frame (Ill. 92-95, 97). Yet even the flat and molded frame members, adorned with carved, engraved and embossed ornamentation, have such a

thoroughgoing rhythm that spatial demarcations such as corners or projecting moldings cause merely accidental interferences having no relationship to the internal form. If in contrast to this one looks at the contemporaneous Florentine creations, a considerable sharpness characterizing the whole comes to the fore. As ornamentation on the flat frame members, softly wreathing loops of creepers, leaves and grotesques are preferred, which in their recurring movements produce complex interlacings. In all designs the contrast between patterned figure and ground is mitigated, so that the internal structure remains restrained (Ill. 81). Typical also are the interruptions of the ornament zones, these latter being crowded together into the centers and corners of the frame members. These subdued "pictorial" effects are then confronted by an accentuation of the flush outer and inner moldings (Ill. 80).

The late Renaissance of the 16th century caused these antitheses to become more pronounced. The Venetians intensified the two-dimensional ornamental border by means of protrusive molding. edges and sweeping contours. Characteristically, these move in most cases differently in the longitudinal and transverse frame members and break out the outside contour to a bizarre silhouette. This form, now known as "Sansovino" frame (Ill. 117-126), is related to the tradition of the upright edicle, and out of the motif of the framing makes an overloaded playful form of the triumphal gates and of the inorganic combination of architectural elements decoratively extended outwards. The Florentine frames, on the other hand, show raised outer edges, in some cases moldings rising steeply from inside to outside (Ill. 82-86). An overelongated egg-and-dart ornamentation appears to stretch like leaf-ends from the projecting edges of the moldings back to the more deeply set inner edge.

The Florentine leaf and volute frames represent a special mannerist variety. They are developed from a combination of acanthus leaves and rolled trim (Ill. 100-103). This type, composed of forms which interchange tensed and smoothly rolled designs one with another without clear-cut demarcation, pushes out the edges of the frame and in fact causes the corners to protrude significantly. The inner leaves are curved forward, the outer backwards. The clear lines and the continuous courses of the design accent the exterior contour; their momentum is carried through in uniform fashion on all edges. The sense of motion which this design conveys helps to unite picture and frame into a single unit. The unreality lies in the material consistency of the delimitation which the frame provides, and not in the composition of the whole, as in Venice.

The art of Bologna contributes something special to the history of frames. Classical tendencies are there in conflict with an inclination to overdone decoration. For a long time the qualities which thus emerged were not recognized. Perhaps the judgment of Wilhelm von Bode contributed to this, for he identified two frame styles which existed parallel to the two decorative tendencies: a dry, academic type and an over-exuberant Baroque type. In this judgment too little attention was given to the fact that these two stylistic tendencies produced results of differing qualitative levels. The early frames have stark outlines, with tilted surfaces set off by narrow profiles. Even the rich, filigree-like ornamentation of the Marchesi Formigine School (Ill. 106-108) is carried out in carefully balanced form and within strict frame proportions. In several specific forms—as, for example, in the lightly pebbled flat frames (Ill. 87-90)—the ornamentation is slightly raised above the surface. A simpler version of this with more pronounced edges was widely produced in the 17th century. In the late 16th and early 17th centuries there occurred mixed types of flat and leaf frames. The relatively broad flat strip in the middle is overlapped nearly up to its center line by protruding leaves, which stem from the middle of the surround. The transition from the edge of the picture to the edge of the frame is thus expressively accentuated, while the surface of the frame remains essentially untouched. The unique quality lies in the leaf-, flower-, fruit-decoration and other details, which are distributed around in such a manner as to form small units of their own. The finely drawn outlines are geometrically simple, and create an impression of fundamental balance (Ill. 110).

The pure leaf frames developed in the 17th century take their starting point from the basic type with accentuated protrusions on the inner side, which then emerge into a projection of continuous leaves placed at right angles to the accent strip. The strength of this form is, however, preserved throughout by the profile which surrounds it on the inside and the outside (Ill. 112-115).

In the second half of the 17th century the open leaf frames arose, frames whose outer boundary—even though broken up into a fine zig-zag line—still remained basically straight. Even the inner boundary preserved a continuous edge in the form of a unified network design. It is the leaf and branch elements which, curving around one another, give motion to this outline (Ill. 195, 197). Even in the high Baroque frames of a slightly later period the movement in the leafy branches remains symmetrical. The structure of the inside frame is differentiated from the decoration and given expression in the form of columns or protrusions (Ill. 196-199).

A typical Roman frame is the "Salvator Rosa" or "Maratta" type, which appeared in the 17th century (Ill. 200, 204-207). It offered a design with a sequence of profiles rising in gradual progression toward the outer edge. Cornice moldings, turned and leaf forms are the hallmarks of this type. In the 18th century the sequence of profile, fluting, profile was modified into a more unifying form, an ogee profile which rose gradually toward the outer edge. This was then decorated with thin ornamental stems, or but lightly stepped. The decorative unity was secured by the ornamental

Fig. 17. Georges Charmeton (1623-74). Engraved designs for frame profiles and ornamentation for use in interior and exterior architecture. *London, Victoria and Albert Museum.*

stems. A variant of this type, characterized by a less pronounced profile, was produced in Naples. (A variation with a markedly classical influence with a suppressed profile sequence is shown in the catalogue of "Italian Picture Frames" produced by the Alte Pinakothek Museum in Munich.) The late Baroque, painted version shows a soft profile, markedly directed toward the outer edge, that after a ledge rises further to a rounded rib. This is separated from a differentiating fluting which in turn is followed by an ogee molding which falls off to the outside edge (Ill. 202)

The Florentine Baroque frames are more plastic than those originating in Bologna. Turned pieces meshed one with another, plus rolled trim, leafy designs and shell forms are voluminously distributed over the surface of the inner frame (Ill. 208, 209, 368). Reference to the mid-point of the surround and to the corners of the frame is characteristic and pronounced. Through their breadth combined with specially compact design, the Florentine frames belong to that category which rates as pathetic and heavy in its impact.

Besides the numerous other design forms — not least those resulting from the influence of the French forms of ornamentation — Venice in particular produced in the late Baroque era several unmistakable types. Among these is the "Canaletto" frame, with its delicate decoration similar to that on mirrors, and with its surface ornamentation of little mirrors and flowers (Ill. 215). A particularly flexible variety is the "Venetian Rococo" frame (Ill. 216, 219), whose tightly intertwined accent decoration is composed of individually expressive designs knitted together into a ribbon-like sequence. Here the irregular natural forms of branches appear, half accidentally, set into a flat profile, with profile pieces intermittently attached on the inside and the outside. No less charming are the small decorative frames with delicate leaf ornamentation on the inside edge (Ill. 222), such as frequently were produced by Pietro Longhi's studio (as can be seen in the Querini-Stampaglia Palace in Venice).

Spanish Frames

Spanish frames exhibited the same general characteristics up to the 16th century. Individual frame designs, such as those of Domenico el Greco, adhere to the Italian tradition of altar framing. In the late 16th century flat frames with sloping ornamentation appeared, joining egg-and-dart and toothed forms with rectangular and rhomboid appliqué. On the base surface of the flat frame with its raised and emphasized profile, these hooks and discs appear as if they had been stapled or nailed on (Ill. 135-138). Many of these in their form of ornamentation have the same effect as an angular variation of the manneristic Florentine frames with their long pipe-stem carvings. Many of the Neapolitan frames of the 17th century cling to this kind of crude and sometimes rough ornamentation (Naples was linked politically with Spain). With the adoption of the flat frame with ornamentation at the corners and in the middle section deriving from Italian art, yet another special variety emerges. The flower and leaf decoration on these is carved and painted, partly in a form rolled outward. Sometimes alternating with painted and engraved patterns on the flat surface, abstract, rolled leaf forms are located between the inclosing profile trim. Silver decoration is typically found on these frames, frequently with gilding of the carved ornamentation (Ill. 145).

Netherlandish, Flemish, and Frames from the Alpine Lands

Among the Dutch frames, we encounter at the end of the 16th and the beginning of the 17th century simple flat frames side by side with more elaborate concepts with a strong Italian influence (Ill. 160). Probably to exhibit an eclectic taste, individual specimens of Italian and French format are included alongside the dark wood frames of the native tradition as more stylish esthetic forms.

The simplest Dutch frames consist of flat dark wooden strips fitted together in a scarf joint (Ill. 157). The typical form, especially for valuable pictures, was trimmed with shining ebony veneer, particularly in the 17th century. Its profile, in the early, simple form, consists of a flattened hollow piping which tips toward the outside; both on the inside and the outside edge it can have one or more steps to it (Ill. 155, 156).

This basic design is repeated two or three times in juxtaposition, separated by flat, running surfaces, in the most elegant German and Alpine frames (Ill. 172-175). Flame-like or wave-like decorations are glued on these flat strips. In proportion to the breadth of the flat surfaces and the profile, these frames resemble the basic type of flat frame. In many examples of frames with richly ornamented flame-like trim, the strongly emphasized profile is turned toward the inside, so that a sequence of ornamented surfaces rises in steps toward the outside. In the case of some exceptionally elegant examples (Ill. 173, 174, 175), the thin profile trim lines separating the flat surfaces are emphasized not merely by the alternation of surface ornamentation, but also by gilding.

The development of the veneer technique using ebony in Flanders and Holland (from which the designation "ebonized," common in the 18th century, derived) took place not on functionally similar frames but rather on furniture cabinets. From the end of the 16th century onward Antwerp was the center of this work. Likewise the inlay technique, using alternating veneer pieces, polished shell fragments and ivory, especially preferred for mirror frames, was developed here. From the framing of the leading edges of cabinets with miniature pictures it is not far to the individual frames (mostly Flemish but also German and Austrian) with inlays of polished shell veneer, the effect not infrequently further enhanced by gold or various other colors (Ill. 163, 164). Still, apart from individual mirror enclosures, the Flemish frames are more restrained in form and ornamentation of their profile (observation of the numerous gallery pictures stemming from the 17th century confirms this).

In the German and the broader Alpine arena, pear wood is used in preference to the scarce and expensive ebony. The production of frames in massive wood pieces containing both structure and ornamentation, and without the use of veneer, is characteristic of the "Alpine" frame frequently described as "Dutch"; these were turned out in great quantity (Ill. 165, 168).

The 17th century in Holland witnessed the conquest of middle class ways of thinking and styles of life in many realms. The ebony wood frame in the sparely carved upper middle class "Regent" style with its resemblance to black Atlas silk can represent this "middle class" type. The unchased, plainly varnished material directs one's attention to the furniture and thereby to the daily life of the domestic furnishings. Specifically through the de-emphasized outline the frame is extended into the room rather than being demarcated from it. The same effect is achieved by the character of the material used, whether elsewhere stressed or made more elegant by paint overlay. This effect is carried so far in the German or Alpine frames as to seem

unreal. The wave and basketweave structure of the polished surface causes the impact of the light to overshadow everything else. The moving reflection of light within the frame surfaces and the dark places which correspond to this merely produce an optical isolation. To be sure, as early as the 15th and 16th centuries comparable dark, flat, one-colored frames had existed, yet these only represented the "economy version" of the richly worked and ornamented types. In their basic, common form, simple edges and profiles were employed for demarcation. But in these "middle class" frames the frequently multiple piping and wavy trim strips merely serve to confuse the juncture of wall surface and picture. The stepping of the flat piping makes it harder to determine whether the picture is behind or in front of specific frame surfaces. Since in this type of frame no other profile and no other ornamentation is present which could be derived from the structural or decorative forms of the architecture, one misses any connection with the symbolic forms through which individual rooms and parts of rooms can be characterized. The black frame, even in the second half of the 17th century, no longer delineates a "representative" content but rather a realm of heightened sense impression. It is directed at intensive absorption and contemplative ramification—without regard to the immediate surroundings.

A comparable type, designed solely with reference to the picture, is to be found again in late romantic estheticism (Ill. 393, 394, 398), in late impressionism (Ill. 418), and in the early phase of Art Nouveau (Ill. 409, 410). The broad surfaces, iridescently finished, with their subordinated geometric interior pieces are common in these later frames. Even the flat and dully painted frames of Marc, Kirchner, Nolde and other expressionists can be seen as a continuation of this kind of frame: it is no accident that the dry Dutch forms foreshadow this (Ill. 157). It is also understandable that the academic and historically oriented painting of the end of the 19th century rediscovered the black Dutch frames for itself. For the "historicism" which had taken over the salons—as a more tasteful combination of popular stylistic forms—lacked any decorative principles deriving from the extension of architectonic objectives.

To the extent that decorative impulses came to the fore in the first half of the 17th century in Holland—in hair styles, in clothes, in decorative furnishings—they took their direction from French, Italian or Flemish models. Formal rooms could thus be decorated in the Italian manner (as for example in Ill. 160) or individual architectural features of Italian or French design could be included, as the frame designs of Rembrandt (Fig. 14) or the painted frames of the Rembrandt-like Holzhacker family (Cassel, Hessian State Museum, Picture Gallery) reveal. A typical Dutch version of the gilded decorated frame first appeared around the middle of the century: in the so-called "Lutma" frame. This introduces relief-like decorations of flowers, masks, emblems, stylized heads and other quite concrete figures and groups of figures on a flat frame trim, and smooths these with muscular and ear-like manipulation of the frame rim. The antecedents of this style, which had a pronounced influence on England and north Germany, are to be found in the manneristic frames of Florence and Venice. Both influences can be seen in an early type (Ill. 160). To these should be added the early stages of the flat frame of the 17th century decorated with emblems (Ill. 158). The communicative wealth of a form with many aspects is not restricted by any clear-cut system of priorities. It appears almost to be playing in its use of irregular wave-like forms embedded in the rim of the frame. There is no constructive relationship between the raised relief-like surfaces of the frame and the inner edge which demarcates the picture. Nothing is visible of the structure and the plasticity of the members of the frame; rather a display board smoothly joined to the picture has emerged with a shield-shaped termination. The decorative features are attached to this from top to bottom, symmetrically on both sides, while the upper edge is fancied up with standing figures. Thus the associative figures rise half-plastic from an amorphous background. The flat gold finish emphasizes the undefined modelling (only the frame edges are polished to a shine, which enables them to demarcate with pencil-like precision). The flat effect, the lack of plasticity and of association with architectural structure is shared with the veneered type of frame.

French Frames

In the light of this background the fundamentally different concept underlying the French frames becomes clear. This is where the development of frame art culminated. Stimulated by the Parisian court art, the most fully developed masterpieces of the art of the frame appeared here between the 17th century and the Napoleonic era. This circumstance arises less from the status of French painting—which only in the 18th century outran all other schools—than from the level achieved by the décor and furnishing accomplishments of, alike, the urban bourgeoisie and the clerical and feudal classes. These sociological underpinnings cannot here be further explored, but it is clear that the forms developed at court spread out into the middle class products of the small towns and countryside. This happened not merely through the individual creations of carvers, cabinet-makers, overlay painters and all other artistic craftsmen, but principally from the patterns (Figs. 18-22) which emanated from France and were equally determinative for all Europe. This cultural uniformity can be traced through all stages of French classicism—from the Louis XVI style up to the Empire—and through a country shaken to its foundations by a Revolution; it should not be confused with social and political harmony. Artistic forms, so much is clear to be seen, always had, in France, a quite different status and acceptance than in Germany, Holland or Italy, where despite all the stimuli provided by the leading art houses, middle class, ecclesiastical and aristocratic forms remained distinct (the particularly varied development occurring in England will be more extensively explored.

In simplified form, it can be said that in France artistic norms accordingly played a rather special role, because pictures and pictorial presentations did not have to portray "reality" directly. The priorities of artistic expression had to emerge clearly in the design concept. The adoption of Renaissance forms during the 16th century was consequently reflected as a dialogue with a set of rules: this is brought out very clearly in the fine "Edicule" frames, which are labelled after the producers of the portraits so frequently displayed in them, "Clouet" or "Corneille of Lyon" frames (Ill. 250, 252). If one compares the products of this group (of which a large number are to be found in the Louvre, in Paris, and in the Koninklijk Museum voor Schone Kunsten, Antwerp) with the earlier Italian types, one is struck by an impression of less spaciousness, as well as a more pronounced incorporation of the foreground. Among the Italians, frames are themselves little architectural creations, whose construction is in one case, the Florentine, based on the statics

Fig. 18. Gille Marie Oppenordt (1672-1742). Design of a frame with coat of arms of the House of Bourbon-Orleans. Pen and ink, c.1730(?). *Paris, Musée des Arts Decoratifs.*

Fig. 19. Nicolas Pineau (1684-1754). Design of a frame. Pen and ink, c.1740. *Paris, Musée des Arts Decoratifs.*

of a building, and in the other, the Venetian, on the dominance of the overshadowing ornamentation. In the French frames, this architectonic form is distinctly separated from the flat surround holding the picture: through either the device of resting the structural members on pedestals which are set at right angles, or that of employing columns which stand in front of the basic frame surface. Through a depressed middle section of the frame pedestal a uniformly deep frame surface is created, distinct from the visually predominant, angularly incorporated architectural elements. Through surrounding ornamental trim and a geometric interior structure—rectangular and round stone inlays and painted variations of ogee and wave patterns—both the levels are, however, held together. Even the optical continuation of the columnar structure in the backwards-looking pedestal and vase additions (or, as in many examples, the continuation of the vertical em-

phasis of the rear frame edge in the inner edge of the outer pediment) effectively ties the surface and the plastic elements together. Expressive forms and functional characteristics are so intertwined in the first impression, while in the second they are seen as in tension with one another.

That which appears to the modern viewer as a "style" which can be altered at will was in fact a form of expression which presumed a prior understanding of a long extant tradition (which, especially in the 16th century, had little flexibility where it involved religious pictures). This was even more true of the French artistic concept, in which the norms of artistic expression were very important, and which inevitably drew on traditional notions. For this reason special interest attaches to two almost contemporary frames commissioned in the same place and by the same party (Ill. 253, 254), respectively in 1518 and 1525, and which incorporate in an "Edicule" form first Renaissance and then late Gothic forms. Comparison of the two and likewise with the miniature frames (Ill. 252) clearly brings out the common basic pattern shared by these architectonic frames: high-rising vertical members with a canopy-like roof joining them, reflecting the canons of Gothic construction.

Fig. 20. Richard de Lalonde. Design of a frame including the Bourbon coat of arms. Pen and ink; dated 1779. *Paris, Private Collection.*

The French secular frames of the 17th century are joined to the architectonic tradition in profile and ornamentation — as are the contemporary Italian picture frames, which are in part the direct precursors of the French. Among the Italian frames of the end of the 16th and the 17th centuries profile and ornamentation incorporate what appears to be an overdone dynamic: individual profile parts are throughout modelled plastically, and stand pronouncedly in front of the frame surface; the ornamentation (particularly in Florence, but also in the flatter frames of Bologna) protrudes in broad and thick layers. On the basis of the functional structure of a frame as an elementary form, a multiplicity of silhouette and profile variations was developed drawing on the repertoire of architectural ornamentation. Each type of frame possesses a different sculptural combination of these elements. In contrast to this, the French frames beginning with the Louis XIII style and continuing up to the end of the 18th century reveal an almost uniform basic design. It corresponds to the surrounding indentation, which mediates between the ceiling and the supporting walls. The French frames are in this sense spatial: their profile turns outward and forms in conjunction with the four side pieces a kind of perspective

Fig. 21 Jean-Aurèle Meissonnier (1693-1750). Design of a frame. Pen and ink; c.1740. *Paris, Private Collection.*

frame for the picture. Within this tectonic structure the employment of ornamentation is predetermined. Delimiting ornamental rods run along the inner and outer edges. In the broad intermediate zone between these two demarcations of picture and wall can be found the richly decorated and mutually interconnected linkage provided by the "piping." This can be stepped and can consist of alternating concave and convex moldings.

The development of the French frame style can be viewed as an expressive adjustment of this basic pattern. The Louis XIII type (Ill. 255, 256, 260) which can be found from the middle of the 17th century onward, is characterized by a close bonding of the ornamentation and the profile and by its rectangularly bounded zones of decoration. In the late phase of this style the ornamental ogee of the profile molding is shifted outward and separated from the inner profile by a flat intermediate zone. The outer profile is increasingly de-emphasized and in part overshadowed by ornamentation, which ties leaf, branch, and flower ornamentation in the Louis XIV style together into a geometric

Fig. 22. Nicolas Pineau. Frame design. Pen and ink; c.1740. *Paris, Musée des Arts Decoratifs.*

web. The succession of mirror-like sequentially or schematically opposing designs is carried over into a rhythmically abstract surface ornamentation of tendrils and streamers. (These transitional forms are to be seen in Ill. 257, 258, 259, 261; mature forms of the Louis XIV style are shown in Ill. 267-269). The outer profile is in these cases partially invisible, because it has been pulled back into the under edge behind the ornamental strips. The ornamentation is put together from vignettes of shield-like surfaces which finally in rolled fashion are elevated into exuding interior planes set off from the surrounding profile. In part the surface structure can be so differentiated—as, for example, by engraving—that small surface units can be raised above the background as a pattern. If one starts from the preconceptions of the basic design, the molded zone of tension between picture and surrounding appears to be extended outward, and as though the rubber-like ornaments which seem to spray forward over the broadened profile are drawn toward the rear. It is important to note how here even the form of ornament is not at first overly expressive, but rather in a kind of artistic manipulation is directed toward the architectonic background. The ornamental material appears at times to accommodate to the outwardly exuding energy, at other times to wall itself off and to roll itself up. This appearance of the natural and unbidden contributes a sense of the highly refined in what is a thoroughly artificial structure.

Besides the form of the uniformly ornamented frame there existed at the end of the 17th century—and thus contemporaneously with the fully developed Louis XIV ornamentation—frames which through their package of corner and intermediate ornamentation carried further the design concepts of the Louis XIII style (Ill. 262-264). Yet in this case there are juxtaposed, and in contrast to one another, what elsewhere seems to be complementary: the strongly molded base of the profile and the flowers and leaves, which in flat design project beyond it.

In contrast to the decreasingly defined, flat and outward-turning form of the bearing profile, the heightened contours of the ornaments seem more and more to carry the emphasis. Even in the Louis XIV frames, in optical impression the interior structure dominates over the exterior form. This imbalance becomes very pronounced in the succeeding period of Regency and Louis XV. Square cartouches as independent spatial elements are situated at an angle over the mitering, and the central ornamentation is emphasized. Among the ornamental forms of the Regency, geometric and symmetric ribbon decoration is a commonly repeated technique. In the interior structure, surface elements (Ill. 272-275) are emphasized, and a pattern of mutually related figures is imposed in contrapuntal fashion over the plastic form. Even in the composition of the surface areas the consciously sought contrast between traditional profile demarcation and emphasized ornamentation is to be found (Ill. 273, 279).

In the Louis XV frames the ornamentation becomes, finally, the carrier of the predominant plastic qualities. Cartouche edging and linking flanges bring together a moving optical structure, as it appears (Ill. 277, 281, 283-290). The still suppressed indication of the basic form in the expressively expanded piping is finally fitted into the movement conveyed by the ornamental flanges (Ill. 289-295). In the transitional phase from the Louis XV style to that of Louis XVI, called the "Transition" (Ill. 291, 293-295), this contrast is reduced to the juxtaposition of the straight trim lines on the inner edge and on the pronounced outer profile. The latter is more strongly stressed than is the inner profile. In the Louis XVI style itself (Ill. 297-315), that is, early classicism, the inner profile again becomes a straight line, well-

Fig. 23. Germain Boffrand (1667-1754). Representation of the wall decorations in the drawing room of the Princesse de Rohan on the second floor of the Hôtel de Soubise, Paris; executed c.1735. *Livre d'architecture,* Paris 1745.

defined in its ornamentation.

The about-face from the fantasy-rich, plastically ornamented forms to the acceptance of the strict classical pattern for the still decorated zones of the frame was based on the already mentioned shift in the conception of the picture. The older pictures had been so perceived that, through their artistic execution, they provided direct insight into the real world. The 18th century adopted this attitude only to a limited degree; in its view reality could be experienced only through its reflection as theater, that is, through the consciousness of its artificiality. The conversion mechanism of the stage had to be made visible, so that the refined fiction could have a real content. The form of the introductory *frame* had to prepare the viewer for something artificial which, however, possessed the logical possibilities contained in the natural world. It is therefore not accidental that wall structures, woodwork and ornamental prints in the 18th century developed their own "artistic categories." These decorations in stucco, wood and paint exhibit the broadest ⸺al effects in residences and in

churches. As the language of mythology and the character of form-determining types could no longer be linked, these references became as fictional as the representative world of. pictures. The truth of artistic forms no longer emerged from the differentiation of artistic and natural characteristics but produced artificial structures, whose criteria had to lie in the realm of esthetics. In this area the prevailing norm was more and more the classicism of the ancient world.

English Frames

The English frames of the 17th century exhibit special features related to those of the "Lutma" frames. Earlier the disc and leaf frames were basically flat (Ill. 227, 231) with Italian-style ornamentation (similar examples can be found in France and Germany). As in Holland, the rolled and muscular decoration of the engraved ornamentation was the model for the frames which convey a sense of motion. The painted example shown in Ill. 227 reveals the pattern behind the carved pieces in Ill. 228-230. The

Fig. 24. Anonymous artist. Sketches of corner and center ornaments of picture frames. Pen drawing in the so-called Knobelsdorff Sketchbook, 1743/44. *Berlin, Verwaltung der Staatl. Schlösser und Gärten.*

Englishman Grinling Gibbons, born in Rotterdam in 1648, was the most gifted creator of this type of ornamentation. The "Sunderland" frames can be regarded as an average example of the "Lutma" and "Vianen" styles, with its more pronounced ornamentation (Ill. 233, 235). Just as the regard for the Dutch painters and their frames was dictated by political circumstances, so the French tendencies fluctuated in like fashion during this period (Ill. 236-241). The frame forms of the Louis XIII style came to dominate after 1660 as a consequence of the Restoration (Charles II was a first cousin of Louis XIV). Similarly, the Dutch influence became more pronounced after the accession of William III of the House of Orange (1689). But within England different regions and different political tendencies produced favored stylistic trends, based upon allegiance to either a royalist taste with French overtones or to a puritan, Dutch style. Further, adaptations of foreign stylistic forms, such as the "Lely" frames, were also possible (Ill. 232). In that case a form of profile was taken over

from the Venetian mirror frames and decorated after the fashion of the late Louis XIII flower ornamentation in discrete carved segments. The overlay was, by preference, silver, but only highly polished in the intermediate zones, that is the flat "mirrors."

The parallel existence in the same time frame of different style forms continued into the 18th century and produced a yet greater richness of variation. For example there is the special form of the Regency (or George I) frames (Ill. 318), a bit later the variety known as the "Maratta" frames (Ill. 326, 327) coexisting with a narrower derivative of the French style. A very extensive version of the French form is represented by the Thomas Chippendale (1709-1779) style. In his furniture, and especially in his mirror frames, this extremely productive creator of decorative cabinetry for England's high society joined Rococo forms with those deriving their inspiration from China and from high Gothic. Even in his picture frame designs and in the executions stylistically related to these (Fig. 1, Ill. 320)

Fig. 25. Anonymous artist. Sketch of a picture frame. Pen and ink; c.1743/44. From the so-called Knobelsdorff Sketchbook. *Berlin, Verwaltung der Staatl. Schlösser und Gärten.*

there can be found much of the overrich fantasy which characterized his thin-walled decorative forms. The adopted form of the Louis XIII style, particularly under the influence of Chippendale's guide, *The Gentleman and Cabinet-Maker's Director* (Ill. 321-324), attached the French forms as a continuous tongue-like ribbon of decoration in a flat plane on the outer edge of the narrow sloping frame structure—a typical example of the adoption of a form without consideration of the expressive consequences. It is significant that in England there is no contemporary development of classicism, as occurs in the French transition stages and those of the Louis XVI frames, but at this time the ancient classical forms of the "Maratta" frames enjoyed a vogue. Just a bit later, from the early '70s on, a neoclassicism made itself felt in the clear outer lines and the similarly decorated surface of the frame with its effect of metallic hardness (Figs. 28, 29, Ill. 328). Along with these there existed examples following the style of the Louis XVI frame as it occurred in France.

Baroque Frames in Other Lands

In the other countries of Europe during the Baroque period there was, just as in England, a dominant influence first of Italian, then of French forms. In the various regions one could find varying interpretations, either more architectural or more ornamental, of the profiles, the ornamentation, and the frame skeleton. The migratory character of the artisan class, without respect to international borders, tended to blur the distinctions among national styles: in the larger workshops, particularly those attached to a court, artisans from every land were at work. For example, in the cabinet-making workshops of the Bavarian court, expanded on a regular basis from 1715 onward, ultimately some 90 craftsmen were at work, among them many Italians. Also the division of labor in the production process brought with it a mixture of influences: the court architect Effner whose ornamental notions followed French patterns (Effner had been trained at the French court and continued to correspond with designers there) dictated the general type, but the profile cutting, the ornamental carving, the en-

46

Fig. 26. Frederick Crace (1779-1859). Designs for wall decoration with chinoiserie frames for the Royal Pavillion at Brighton, 1810-20. Pen and watercolor. *New York, Cooper-Hewitt Museum.*

Fig. 27. John Linnell. Design for hanging frames of varying oval shapes. Pen and ink; dated 1778. From Linnell's Album. *London, Victoria and Albert Museum.*

Fig. 28.   John Linnell. Design for a frame in the style of Louis XVI. Pen, pencil and watercolor. From Linnell's Album; c.1778. *London, Victoria and Albert Museum.*

Fig. 29.   Robert Adam (1728-92). Design for the frame of the portrait of the Duke of Cumberland. London, Home House, 1777. *London, Courtauld Institute of Art.*

graving and the gilding were carried out by other hands, in each case. The series of frames prepared in such workshops for particular sequences of castles and the contemporary gallery displays (Ill. 356-362) reveal variations not merely of profile and ornamentation, but also in the quality of the execution, which can be traced both to the nature of the assorted commissions and to the differences in the caliber of the workmen. (Unfortunately the local origin of respective frames has hardly been researched; even in galleries with a large collection of old frames, the connection with the picture for which the frame was intended has seldom been preserved.)

In the Germanic countries, there is to be found throughout a diffusion of the expressive stimulus given by the French style of ornamentation. Even in the systematically designed "Effner" frames one is struck, in making comparisons with similar French examples, by the exclusive flat form of the corner ornamentation derived from the corner cartouche. Compact, sharply tilted ornamental leaves overlap a gently curved profile. Its exterior contour is not optically segregated by any added profile or by any ornamental flange. The linear emphases focus attention on the inner edge of the frame or in some cases its inner profile more than on

the outer contour. This connection between the body of the profile trim and the markedly curved "ears" of the corner cartouche is retained in French provincial frames. By contrast, the ornamental forms of the "Effner" frames portray a combination of more abstract influences: the non-three dimensional border strips of the picture terminate in a kind of spring clasp (Ill. 357, 360); the converging linear energy seems to push the corners outward at an angle, and to concentrate the movement of the ornamentation at that point. One can differentiate two phases in which this form of corner was employed: an earlier one utilizing the replacement of the profile through an overshadowing system of successive flanges (Ill. 356, 358, 359, 361) and a later one, in which the corners bend dynamically outward (Ill. 357, 360, 362). Both share the tendency to override the sharp delimitation of the inner edge on its outer side with a structure of symmetrical relations and organic mergers. The dynamic which unfolds itself from the edge of the picture outward adopts in particular the decorative forms of ribbon design and then of the rocaille. By this means the frame surface can be given the quality of an amorphous, disembodied film of streaming motion. The most fantastic culmination of this procedure is to be found in the work of the Nahl and the Hoppenhaupt circle (Ill. 338-340), and in Bavarian and Austrian church Rococo (Ill. 329). The interpretations differ according to whether the energy embodied in the corners seems to stream outward, break off, or be dammed up. A very refined version is to be found in the muscled corner treatment of the Danish frames (Ill. 341, 343).

Frame Styles since the 19th Century

A new concept of "Art" is linked to the classicist frames with their overtones suggestive of antiquity. On the one hand the works included in this category carry further themes deriving from outmoded notions of theology, morality and political theory. These prescribed the placement of picture and frame on particular walls. The newer esthetics of the Enlightenment, by contrast, rejected the use of art for extraneous purposes of any kind. On the subconscious level of the emotions a new world of meaning was created. Perceptions cleansed of everything but pure esthetics were detached from notions of interior design: there was no longer any link between the message of the picture and particular persons, classes, interiors or types of rooms. If either the artist or the viewer desired to demarcate a purely esthetic zone of perception, then it was the function of the frame to separate this sphere from the everyday world around it. Indeed, this was felt to be valid for all pictures of all eras. One could no longer—as one could in the Baroque era—link the expressive form of the frame with a specific expressive concept of the relevant contemporary pictures and their style relationship to the frame. Consequently the frame became a piece of interior décor, whose form was determined by general esthetic notions, in the same fashion as were other elements of interior design.

The stylistic development of the 19th century shows what had, in each period, served as the essence of "classic" or "artistic" form: first the decoration reminiscent of the world of antiquity (Ill. 381, 382, 385, 386), then a return to Gothic forms (Ill. 379, 389), and finally a late Baroque (Ill. 390-392) reduced to surface ornamental etching. The ornamentation in each case was, on the basis of the process used, adaptable and capable of repetition, since it was normally produced through negative model forms. Aside from the overall flatter effect of this decoration, these frames frequently also possessed a flat intermediate zone between the edge of the picture and the inner edge of the frame; they didn't start out with a profile, as did the classical types. In the second half of the century, and especially in the reemployment of historic frames, this intermediate zone became a broad "cuff" (Ill. 397, 399).

Artists with a highly developed philosophy of the life of culture, such as the English pre-Raphaelites, laid down their own stylistic rules for their frames, which they consciously viewed as flat hems or borders (Ill. 393-396). The search for original forms was thus directed toward non-European models (Ill. 395, 398). Finally historicism cultivated a special purity of esthetic form, in which it was sought to imitate the historic forms of the profile structure together with its ornamentation, and with stylistic precision, as in the artistic Florentine frames of the 19th century (Ill. 401-403). Art Nouveau took seriously the notion of a surrounding decorative zone, in the sense that flat pieces took the place of the profile, the concept of a surrounding design was given up, and any desired structure could be appliquéd (Ill. 407-415). Thus prominent parts of the picture could be reproduced on the frame, or figures created by fantasy, or calligraphic designs. In many cases, nothing more was done than to nail thin pieces of profile trim on the broad edge of the picture canvas, the intermediate spaces being painted. It is understandable that in the face of such variable forms of framing many new uses were found for old frames, especially those with a folk art type of decoration suggestive of exotic themes (Ill. 420-422). The historical structure of the frame, now become meaningless, was treated as wholly lacking in content, a neutral but charming addendum. The French impressionists took battered Baroque frames of undistinguished execution, whose gilding had been poorly preserved, and simply painted them over in bright colors: this practice, with its still operative nostalgic effect (Ill. 417), made tasteful the decayed condition of historic survivals. The same esthetic approach underlies the use of rustic Spanish and Italian Baroque ornamentation for the framing of exotic forms of modern art (Ill. 445, 446).

Conclusion

The unique character of historic forms gives an undeniable charm to old picture frames. Where a form has been developed in a rich and clear design, it so claims the attention that it is difficult to relate it to a similarly executed artistic creation, such as an old picture. Fancy historic frames have the same effect as do the frames of prints and mirrors, or quite alone engender satisfaction for the modern taste.

Yet for an understanding of the historic background it is essential to view pictures in their proper or at least in closely related frames. This embedment in the last survivor of a long departed spatial concept better helps us to reach back into that comprehensive view of pictures and drawings which is found at the origins of our culture and which since then has generated a practically unlimited number of new pictorial forms.

Fig. 30. William Holman Hunt (1827-1910). Studies for the ornamental borders of a portal for the Mosque of Sakrah in Palestine (detail). Pencil. *England, Private Collection; on loan to the Ashmolean Museum in Oxford.*

1 Antique models for ornamentation and profile: Portico of S. Zeno Chapel in S. Prassede, Rome, dating from the second century A.D., reused and newly ornamented on its bottom by Carolingian artisans under Pascalis I (817-824 A.D.).

2 Rounded arch frame with ornamental vine; stucco border, formerly gilded. Presumably frame of the portrait of a mummy. Roman; from Hawara, Egypt, second century A.D.

Antecedents

3   Braided border. Detail from the choir railing of the Basilica, Aquileja, Italy. Stonemasonry work, c.600-700 A.D.

4   Ornamental vine in embossed gold foil. Detail of the antependium in the minster of Basel, c.1020. *Paris, Musée de Cluny.*

5   Polychrome frame of a miniature; possibly imitation of a channel molding. St. John the Evangelist in the coronation evangelium of Charlemagne. Aix-la-Chapelle, c.800. *Vienna, Hofburg, Worldly Treasure Chamber.*

6 Free-standing frame type: "Triumphant Ruler." Detail from an ivory lid. Carolingian, 9th-10th century. *Florence, Museo Nazionale del Bargello.*

7 Horizontal frame type: Scenes from the Crucifixion and Resurrection. Ivory. Carolingian, c.870. From the cover of the Pericope volume of Henry II. *Munich, Bayerische Staatsbibliothek.*

8 Acanthus leaf as related to sacred decoration. Gold foil and filigree work in the representation of the temples of the celestial Jerusalem. Carolingian, c.870. Detail from the cover of the *Codex Aureus* from St. Emmeran. *Munich, Bayerische Staatsbibliothek.*

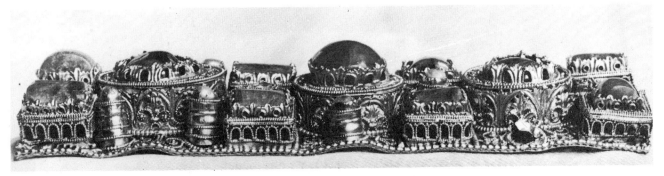

9 Retable of the Soest altarpiece. Early 13th century. *Berlin-Dahlem, Gemäldegalerie.*

10 Quadrifolium frame within a cassette square of the southern bronze door of the Baptistery in Florence by Andrea Pisano, c.1330.

11 Quadrifolium frame. Florence, c.1330-40. Detail from the door of a reliquary in the sacristy of S. Croce. Originally the painting "St. Francis Offering to be Tested by Fire to the Sultan" by Taddeo Gaddi (? -1366) was part of this reliquary. *Munich, Bayerische Staatsgemäldesammlungen.*

12 Profiles of the inner frame of "Madonna Rucellai." Florence, S. Maria Novella, Duccio di Buoninsegna (1255-1319), 1285. *Florence, Uffizi.*

13 Right wing of the main altarpiece of the Stiftskirche in Oberwesel. Viewed when open. Rhine Valley, 1331.

14 Lunette frame for an "Angel" by Guarentieno di Arpo. Formerly part of the decorations of the Carrarese Chapel in S. Agostino. Padua, c.1345-50. *London, Christie's Sale,* 29 March 1974.

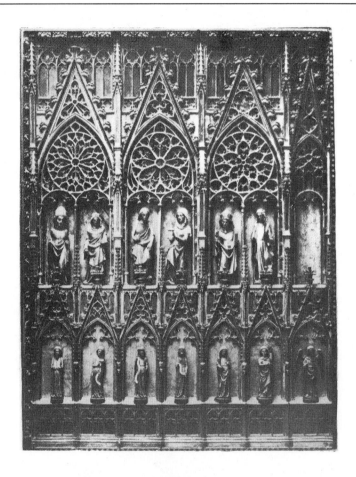

15 Frame construction of the "Adoration of the Magi Altarpiece" by Gentile da Fabriano (1360/70-1427).
Florence, 1423. *Florence, Uffizi.*

16 Detail of fig. 15.

17 Triple Gable frame of the "Crucifixion" by Francesco di Vannuccio. Siena; signed and dated 1370. *Berlin-Dahlem, Gemäldegalerie.*

18 Framed Triptych, attributed to Lorenzo Veneziano, executed between 1370 and 1390 (total height 83 cm.). *London, Christie's Sale,* 2 July 1976.

Architectonic Frames

19 Exterior of the right wing of an altarpiece; the so-called "Worms Panel." Rhine Valley, c.1260. Picture and frame from the same piece of wood. *Darmstadt, Hessisches Landesmuseum.*

20 Gold-trimmed interior of fig. 19.

21 Gilded frame (silver plated on the sides) of "Virgin and Child," attributed to a follower of Simone Martini (c.1285-1344). Siena, between 1330-1340. *Berlin-Dahlem, Gemäldegalerie.*

22 Gilded frame with embossed plate interposed between profiles for a painting by Paolo di Giovanni Fei. Siena, 1390-1400. *Washington, National Gallery of Art.*

Architectonic Frames

23 Gilded frame. Detail of the center panel of the "Passion Altarpiece" by Master Bertram. Between 1390 and 1400. *Hanover, Niedesächsische Landesgalerie.*

24 Embossed gold frame (tablets and bows) for a "Pietà with Angel." South Germany, c.1490. *Kaufbeuren, St. Blasius Chapel.*

25 Painted frame for the interior of a diptych. Cologne, c.1350. *Berlin-Dahlem, Gemäldegalerie.*

Architectonic Frames

26 Frame with oblique recess, decorated with varicolored stampings. Interior of the right wing of the "Apocalypse Altarpiece" by a follower of Master Bertram. c.1400. *London, Victoria and Albert Museum.*

27 Flat frame grooved along the inner border and decorated with floral ornaments applied with a stamp. Interior of the left wing of the "St. Catherine Altarpiece" in St. Georgen ob Murau (Styria), c.1450.

28 Detail of an engraved and gilded frame, seen from the exterior of the right inside wing between "The Wedding at Cana" and "The Adulteress before Christ" of the St. Wolfgang Altarpiece, Austria. By Michael Pacher (1435-98) and his workshop, 1471-81.

29 Picture frames of the Norfolk Triptych (height 33 cm.), opened. Bishopric Liège, Belgium, c.1415. *Rotterdam, Museum Boymans-van Beuningen.*

30 Original frame of Albrecht Dürer's "Four Apostles." Nuremberg, 1526, gilding renewed. Executed in the manner of wings for an altarpiece. The frame served at the same time as support for the horizontal boards of the panel. *Munich, Alte Pinakothek.*

31 Detail from the ornamental frame of the "Maria Gail Altarpiece," Carinthia. Vines, Birds, and Wild Men, 1515-20.

32 Painted (restored) bramble ornamentation on one of the wings of the "Hohenwang Altarpiece." Styria, c.1520.

33 Marbelized frame (both verso and recto), wood. The original frame belongs to the portrait of Margarete van Eyck, painted by Jan van Eyck (c.1390-1441), 1439. *Bruges, Groeninge Museum.*

34 Imitation stone frame, within an illusionistic painted border. The verso is also marbelized. "Virgin Annunciate"
from a diptych with the representation of the Annunciation by Jan van Eyck, 1430-35. *Lugano, Thyssen Collection.*

35 Frame seen in profile with original hinge of the original frame of the "Monforte Altarpiece" by Hugo van der Goes
(1437/40-82), 1470-75. *Berlin-Dahlem, Gemäldegalerie.*

36 Original arched frame of a "Virgin and Child" by Hugo van der Goes, c.1465. About thirty years later it became part of a triptych with a rectangular center panel. *Frankfurt, Städelsches Kunstinstitut.*

37 Verso of fig. 38 showing the connection of the structural members of the frame and the manner of securing the panel by means of a stave.

38 Imitation stone frame (painted and inscribed) of the portrait of Gilles Joye by Hans Memling (c.1433-94), 1472. *Williamstown, Mass., Sterling and Francine Clark Art Institute.*

39 Frame and panel made from one piece of wood for an "Annunciation." Upper Rhine Valley, c.1420. *Winterthur, Switzerland, Oskar Reinhart Collection.*

40 Late Gothic Tyrolean frame with wide concave grooving. Indentations on the sides indicate that the frame was
  formerly endowed with hinges for no longer extant wings. (The picture did not belong to this frame originally).
  Munich, Bayerische Staatsgemäldesammlungen.

41 Detail of fig. 40: old eyelet for a draw-curtain.

42 Original Profile frame for a North German portrait, c.1480. *Lugano, Thyssen Collection.*

43 Plate frame with deep oblique profile. The oblique area is gilded. Formerly it held a South German portrait on canvas, dated 1542. *Munich, Bayerische Staatsgemäldesammlungen.*

44 Plate frame with attached gilded knobs. It formerly held a painting by a member of the Cranach Workshop, c.1540. *Munich, Pfefferle Collection.*

45 Profile frame with inscription. Right half of a diptych. Originally part of "Mater Dolorosa" by Hans Holbein the Elder (1460/70-1524). Augsburg, 1493. *Berlin-Dahlem, Gemäldegalerie.*

46 Plate frame. Right wing of a double portrait. Originally companion piece of the portrait of Hans Plattner (d. 1562). Nuremberg, dated 1525. *Nuremberg, Germanisches Nationalmuseum.*

Secular Frames North of the Alps

47 Outside frame painted in simulated brick. Inner frame gilded and painted with illusionistic overlap of the hand and the falcon's tail. Portrait of Engelbert II, Count of Nassau-Dillenburg (1451-1504) by the Master of the Prince's Portrait, dated 1482. *Amsterdam, Rijksmuseum.*

48 Alteration of the frame to enhance the illusionistic effect of the lower border. The outer border has been flattened to create a peep-show effect. Center panel of a triptych by Simon Marmion (1425-89). Valenciennes, c.1470. *Lugano, Thyssen Collection.*

77

49 Illusionistic overlapping of a rug. Detail from the left wing of the "Death of the Virgin Altarpiece" by Joos van Cleve (c.1485-1540). Antwerp, c.1520. *Munich, Bayerische Staatsgemäldesammlungen.*

50 Tomblike Arched Profile frame with flat, stagelike border. Original frame of the "Wedding Portrait" by the Master of Frankfurt. Netherlandish, dated 1496. *Antwerp, Konincklijk Museum voor Schone Kunsten.*

51 Diptych of two trifoil arched panels (overall height 36 cm.). Inscribed with the titles of the 16-year old Philip the Handsome and his sister, 14-year old Margaret of Austria. c.1494. *Vienna, Kunsthistorisches Museum.*

52 Triptych with the portraits of the future Charles V and his sisters Eleonore and Isabella. The frame consists partly of flat, partly of profile members. Malines, 1502. *Vienna, Kunsthistorisches Museum.*

53 Venetian Tabernacle frame with pilasters, c.1500. *Oxford, Ashmolean Museum.*

54 Venetian Tabernacle frame with *pastiglia* ornamentation which was formerly gilded. In the superimposed disks
    are etched designs. Early 16th century. *Venice, Ca d'Oro.*

55 Venetian Tabernacle frame flanked by architectural columns. The decorations are partly etched or in *pastiglia*. Late 15th century. *Venice, Ca d'Oro.*

56 Venetian Tabernacle frame with base and etched ornaments. Late 15th century. *Venice, Ca d'Oro.*

57 Tabernacle frame without base. Florence, c.1500-20. *Munich, Bayerische Gemäldesammlungen.*

58 Explanatory illustration: Front view of a tabernacle with symbolic motifs, made of metal foil (the door is missing). Cf. similar tabernacle construction in marble by Desiderio da Settignano (1408-1464), c.1464 in S. Lorenzo, Florence. *London, Victoria and Albert Museum.*

59 Tondo formed from a single convex wreath. The panel is a *desco da parto,* a painted round platter used to serve meals to a woman lying-in. A woman in that condition is shown on the left of the panel. It explains the humble wreath. Attributed to Domenico di Bartolo. Siena, 1425-30. *Berlin-Dahlem, Gemäldegalerie.*

Italian Renaissance Frames

60 Tondo, formed out of an inner and an outer profile rim with superimposed wreath of fruit. This frame formerly held "Madonna with Child" by Luca Signorelli (1445/50-1523). The frame was made in Florence, c.1495. *Munich, Bayerische Staatsgemäldesammlungen.*

61 Tondo, formed out of an inner and an outer profile rim and a carved ornamental center band, of which portions are repeated in mirror image and four medallions are interposed. The frame formerly held "Madonna and Child with St. John and an Angel" from the workshop of Sandro Botticelli (c.1445-1510). Florence, c.1490. A contemporary inscription on the verso of the frame, *M. Giuliano da San Ghallo,* is thought to give the name of the frame-maker. *London, National Gallery.*

62 Tondo, formed from an inner and outer profile rim and a superimposed, carved center band with tracery of masks and birds, partially repeated in mirror image, and interrupted by three dimensional medallions, representing heads of prophets. This frame originally held "The Holy Family" by Michelangelo (1475-1564). It was made by Antonio Barile (1453-1516), a native of Siena. *Florence, Uffizi.*

63   Aediculary frame surrounding the triptych by Giovanni Bellini (c.1430-1516). Built and signed by Jacopo
da Faenza, dated 1488. *Venice, S. Maria Gloriosa dei Frari.*

64   Integral frame of a sculptural group: "The Virgin with the Infant Christ and St. Ann" by Hans Leinberger.
      1513. *Ingolstadt, Gnadenthal Convent.*

64a   Project Drawing by Albrecht Dürer (1471-1528) for the integral frame of the "Landauer Altarpiece," dated 1508. *Chantilly, Musée Conde.*

65   Frame for Albrecht Dürer's "Landauer Altarpiece," carved by Veit Stoss (1445-1535). 1511. *Nuremberg, Germanisches Nationalmuseum.*

Italian Renaissance Frames

66   Inner frame with rounded top. Originally meant for "Venus and Cupid" by Jan Gossaert, called Mabuse (c.1475-1533/36), dated 1520. The inscribed outer frame was probably added shortly after that date. *Brussels, Musées Royaux des Beaux-Arts.*

67   Epitaph-like frame. From the workshop of Peter Flötner (1485-1564). Nuremberg, c.1530. Formerly *Ansbach, Church of St. Gumbert.*

90

68   Plate frame with rounded top and high inside and outside edges. Originally used for a "Charity" of a series
of the cardinal virtues by Maerten van Heemskerck (1498-1574). c.1540. *Vienna, Kunsthistorisches
Museum.*

Polychrome Frames

69   Frame for a triptych with suspended arches forming structural components of the picture area. "Descent from the Cross" and twenty small panels in the flanking pillars by Fra Angelico (1387-1455), c.1437-40. The three triangular panels on top are by Lorenzo Monaco (1372-1412), c.1410-20. *Florence, Museo di San Marco.*

70   Tabernacle frame. Decorated by the Master of the Carrand Madonna. c.1450/60. *Amsterdam, Rijksmuseum.*

71   Devotional painting with painted decoration depicting God the Father and angels with the instruments of Christ's martyrdom. Grisaille. "Calvary" by Frans Francken the Elder (1581-1642), Antwerp, c.1630. *Sale, Kunsthaus am Museum, Cologne,* 16 March 1977.

Polychrome Frames

72   Frame in the manner of an ornamental engraving with cartouches surrounding a "Vanitas" painting of the School of Antwerp. Attributed to F. Pourbas the Younger (1570-1622). *Le Puy, Musée Crozatier.*

73   Frame decorated with cherubs and angels with the instruments of Christ's martyrdom, supplementing the panel, depicting "Madonna and Child," ascribed to Lazzaro Bastiani (c.1430-1512), to enhance devotion. The coat-of-arms is probably that of the Berilacquas of Verona. Anonymous Italian master, c.1460-70. *Berlin-Dahlem, Gemäldegalerie.*

74   Painted frame for a "Last Judgment." Frame and painting by Pieter Huys (1519-84). Some of the demon motifs are modified on the frame (see the enlarged details nos. 75 and 76). *Brussels, Musées Royaux des Beaux-Arts.*

75-76   Details of no. 74.

77 Plate frame from Siena for "Portrait of a Young Woman" by Neroccio de' Landi (1447-1500). Heads of eagles biting golden spheres, alternating with flames, decorate the cassette-like areas. These emblems point to the Bandini family of Siena. c.1490. *Washington, National Gallery.*

78 Plate frame from Siena. Supposedly by Antonio Barile (1453-1516), c.1500. *Siena, Museo del Seminario Arcivescovile.*

79 Plate frame from Siena with ornamental vines and masks, and emblems in the lateral members. Presumably made to frame a portrait. Early 16th century. *Munich, Riggauer.*

80 Plate frame from Florence with shallow profiles and painted ornamental vines (cf. no. 84). End of the 16th century. *Munich, Bayerische Gemäldesammlungen.*

81 Detail from no. 80.

Italian Regional Frames

82   Plate frame from Florence with engraved ornaments and rosettes. The inner edge is adorned by profile rods, the outer edge by foliage. Mid-16th century. *Vienna, Kunsthistorisches Museum.*

83   Plate frame from Florence with high cornice. The inner profile is gilded and adorned with a pearl rod. The principal plate has a pipe-like ornament, drawn upward toward the exterior. The gilt tips and rods contrast with the dark color of the walnut wood. Leaf ornaments are in the corners. *Munich, Bayerische Gemälde-sammlungen.*

84 Plate frame from Florence, richly profiled, with painted decorations in black and gold. The interior and exterior profiles are both stepped down. The outer profile extends over a round gilded rod and a deep cornice, decorated with a painted tooth-like pattern. The front and rear portions are joined by a gusset. *Munich, Bayerische Gemälde-sammlungen.*

85 Plate frame from Florence greatly profiled with painted decorations. The strong profiles are stepped down and alternate with shallow cornices, with a beak-like outer edge. Second half of the 16th century. *Rome, Pinacoteca Vaticana.*

Italian Regional Frames

86   Molding frame from Florence. It is stepped down with an ogee, cut in pipe design. Mid-16th century. *Munich, Bayerische Gemäldesammlungen.*

87   Plate frame from Bologna. Wide gilded plate with embossed rosettes and bell-shaped blossoms and strongly emphasized border molding. The inside profile with cornice and round rod. The outer profile is heightened by being stepped up. *Munich, Bayerische Gemäldesammlungen.*

88   Plate frame from Bologna. Gilded plate with embossed leaf and blossom ornaments. The inner profile is made
of a spiral rod; the outer one of a pearl rod and flat round rod. *Munich, Bayerische Gemäldesammlungen.*

Italian Regional Frames

89   Plate frame from Bologna. Gilded plate, embossed with ornamental areas in the corners and centers
       The inner profile is stepped up toward a half-round rod; the outer one toward a quarter-round rod. Beginning
       of the 17th century. *Munich, Bayerische Gemäldesammlungen.*

90   Detail of no. 89.

91 Plate frame from Bologna. Embossed, gilded plate. Carved leaf ornament superimposed in the corners and centers. The inner profile combines vines and a spiral rod. The outer one is decorated with carved blossoms alternating in direction. *Bologna, Pinacoteca Nazionale.*

92 Pastiglia braid pattern. Detail of the upper horizontal member of a tabernacle frame (cf. no. 99). Venice, first half of the 16th century. *Munich, Bayerische Gemäldesammlungen.*

93 Detail of the corner of a tabernacle frame with embossed ornaments and laminated pastiglia decoration (cf. no. 92). *Munich, Bayerische Gemäldesammlungen.*

Italian Regional Frames

94 – 96   Venetian pastiglia frames. Made from moldings with laterally limited profiles enclosing convex braided or vine patterns which were originally gilded. Dowel holes in the vertical member of no. 94 indicate that it was formerly attached to additional structural members. Venice, early 16th century. *Munich, Bayerische Gemäldesammlungen.*

97   Venetian plate frame. Carved plate with shingled rosettes and carved profile. Second half of the 16th century.
      Munich, Bayerische Gemäldesammlungen.

98   Venetian plate frame with gilded pastiglia superimposed. First half of the 16th century. *Venice, Cà d'Oro.*

99 Venetian plate frame with carved plate and shingled rosettes and carved profiles (foliage, spiral rod, leaf-rod). c.1600. *Munich, Bayerische Gemäldesammlungen.*

100 Leaf frame from Florence with large leaves arranged in two levels, an inner wreath of narrow oblique leaves and scrollwork, and an outer one, recessed, with perforated scrollwork. c.1600. *Munich, Bayerische Gemäldesammlungen.*

101   Leaf frame from Florence (see description on preceding page).

102   Leaf frame from Florence. The intertwining scrollwork is here even more prominent. The inner profile consists of a spiral rod, interrupted by the leafwork. c.1620. *Munich, Bayerische Staatsgemäldesammlungen.*

103 Leaf frame from Florence. Originally belonging to "Judgment of Paris" by Coccapani (1583-1642). c.1620. *Stuttgart, Staatsgalerie.*

Italian Regional Frames

104   Medallion. Detail from no. 105.

105   Luxury frame from Florence in the manner of a plate frame with painted medallions in grisaille, stylistically closely akin to Giorgio Vasari (1511-1574). It is not known which subject this frame was originally intended for. Early in the 19th century, it held a Florentine "Cleopatra." Subsequently it was used to frame the portrait of Giovanni de' Medici by Angelo Bronzino (1503-1572), painted c.1550. The frame dates from c.1550/60. *Oxford, Ashmolean Museum.*

106 Altar frame with carved ornaments from S. Giovanni in Monte, Bologna. Made by Andrea Marchesi da Formigine (1483-1520) for Raphael's "St. Cecilia" of c.1517. *Bologna, Pinacoteca Nazionale.*

107-108   Plate frames from Bologna with carved ornaments in the manner of Marchesi Formigine. Second half of the 16th century. *Bologna, Pinacoteca Nazionale.*

109   Plate frame from Bologna with widened profile along the inner edge. c.1600. *Bologna, Pinacoteca Nazionale.*

110 Leaf frame from Bologna. Beginning with the inner border, the sequence of ornamentation is a *kymation,* spiral rod, leaf pattern, all directed towards the centers of the four members. The inner plate is slanted towards the outside, covered with carved blossom and leaf patterns. A groove separates the outside border, which latter is in the form of a leaf-rod. First half of the 14th century. *Bologna, Pinacoteca Nazionale.*

111 Plate frame from Bologna with rounded top. Decorated with carved interwoven undulations surrounding rosettes. Originally made for Francesco Albani's "Baptism of Christ" altarpiece. Beginning of the 17th century. *Bologna, Pinacoteca Nazionale.*

112   Plate frame from Bologna. Decorated with acanthus leaves, extended and broadened downward except for the tips which are again turned upward. First half of the 17th century. *Bologna, Pinacoteca Nazionale.*

113-15   Transitional forms of Bolognese plate frames toward leaf frames. First half of the 17th century. *Bologna, Pinacoteca Nazionale.*

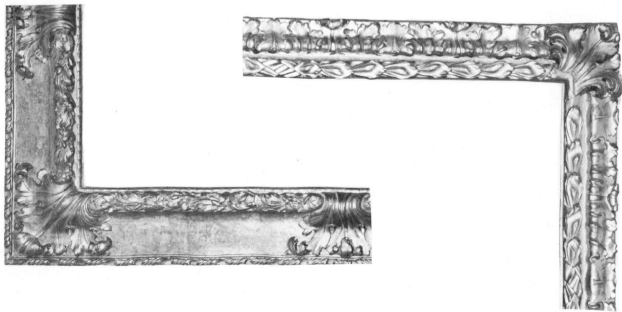

116 Plate frame with extensive carved ornamentation, probably Bolognese, in the manner of Formigine. Formerly in the possession of the Taverna family, Lombardy. Second half of the 16th century. *London, Victoria and Albert Museum.*

117 Venetian frame with interlaced scrollwork, the so-called "Sansovino frame." Early type of a geometrical arrangement of interrupted exterior borders. *Florence, Palazzo Vecchio.*

118 Sansovino frame. In the horizontal members are drawn out volutes; in the vertical parts, hanging and extended. Fish-scale and foliage ornamentation in gold on black background. End of 16th century. *London, National Gallery.*

119   Sansovino frame. End of the 16th century. *London, Victoria and Albert Museum.*

120   Sansovino frame. Profusely carved luxury frame with volute ornamentation and figural decorations. The upper molding is in the form of a ledge below a divided gable. The lower molding in the form of a pedestal. The crown above the top center is no longer extant. Second half of the 16th century. *Munich, Bayerische Gemäldesammlungen.*

121   Sansovino frame with tabernacle structure in small format. Early architectonic configuration. The painting
       is not the original one for which this frame was made. Mid-16th century. *London, National Gallery.*

122 Lower edge of a Sansovino frame. The lateral strips are gilded; the other parts are painted brown. This is a relatively early type with emphatic scrollwork. Mid-16th century. *Munich, Bayerische Staatsgemäldesammlungen.*

123 Detail of carved volute ornaments of a Sansovino frame. Early, strictly geometric scrollwork. Mid-16th century. *Munich, Bayerische Gemäldesammlungen.*

124 Sansovino frame with volute ornamentation and *karyatides*. Coarse execution of the delicate transition of the ornaments. Late type; c.1600. *Munich, Bayerische Gemäldesammlungen.*

125 Sansovino frame with volute and *karyatides*. Coarse execution of the unencumbered volute edges of the small frame. Late style. *London, Pollak Collection.*

126 Venetian provincial variant of a Sansovino frame. The original architectonic elements have been partially misunderstood: the supporting members have become lanterns. 17th century. *Patmos, Convent of St. John.*

127 Neapolitan plate frame with coarsely carved profile. The gilded ornamentation contrasts with the black ground. The inner profile projects greatly, emphasized by the deep grooving. Second half of the 16th century. *Munich, Bayerische Staatsgemäldesammlungen.*

128 Neapolitan plate frame. The profiles are coarse; the outer one is adorned with painted rectangles, black on gold. Second half of the 16th century. *Munich, Riggauer.*

129 Neapolitan plate frame. The inner profile is unusually wide, turned outward, and decorated with pipe-like ornaments. *London, National Gallery.*

130 Spanish plate frame with polychrome decoration in dark green and gold. Calligraphy and ornamentation simulate etching. Castile, second third of the 16th century. *Berlin, Lemke.*

131 Spanish plate frame. Dark brown wood with superimposed ornamentation in honey gilt. Last third of the 16th century. *Berlin, Lemke.*

Spanish, Portuguese, and Latin American Frames

132 Spanish plate frame. Polychrome with gold and silver. Red and green painted ornaments. Mid-17th century. *Berlin, Lemke.*

133 Spanish plate frame with painted ornamentation in black and ochre. Castile, first half of the 16th century. *Berlin, Lemke.*

134 Spanish plate frame with carved ornaments; the corner ornaments are etched; with tortoise shell imitation in the plate surfaces. End of the 16th century/beginning of the 17th century. *Private Collection.*

135 Spanish plate frame with indented exterior edges. Second half of the 16th century. *Munich, formerly Riggauer.*

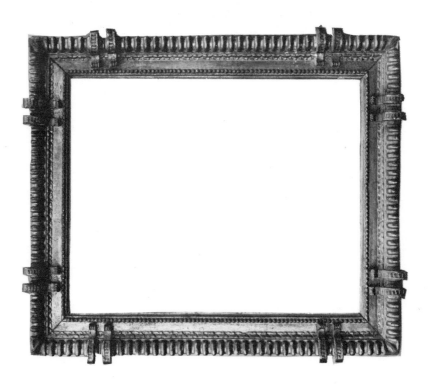

Spanish, Portuguese, and Latin American Frames

136 Spanish plate frame with sumptuous sequence of profiles. The plate is adorned with carved, diamond-shaped ornaments, alternating with other configurations, simulating precious stones. Along the outer edge clamp-like pieces of wood have been attached. Gilded in its entirety. Last third of the 16th century. *Washington, National Gallery.*

137 Spanish plate frame. Three-dimensional ornaments in the shape of precious stones are here surrounded by filagree decoration on a brown base. The clamp-like ornaments along the outer edge are gilded. Last third of the 16th century. *London, Agnew's.*

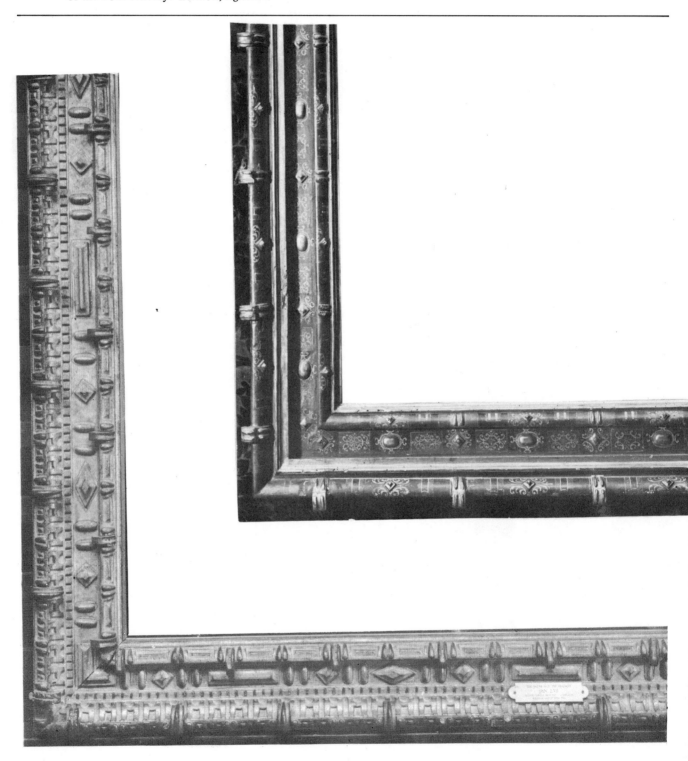

138 Detail of the corner of a Spanish plate frame. The plate in grayish blue with half-round gilded edge. According to an annotation on the verso, this frame was used in a church chamber in northern Spain. Last third of the 16th century. *Munich, Bayerische Staatsgemäldesammlungen.*

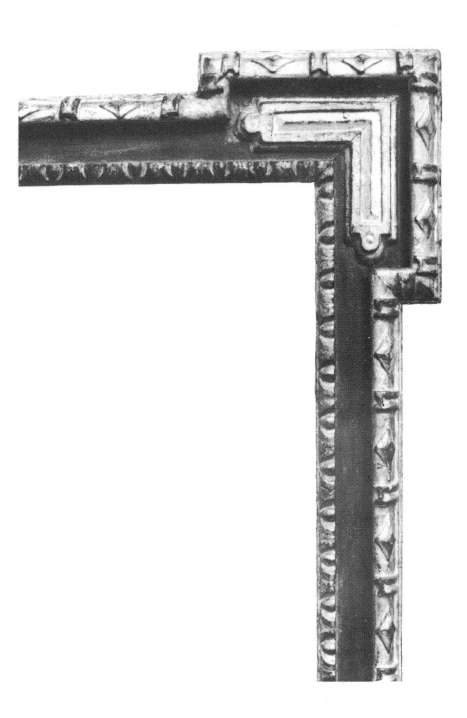

139   Spanish plate frame. Stylized carnation-like ornaments in blue and ochre on a red base. The center of the plate is silver.

140 Spanish plate frame with carved leaf ornaments, gilded in the corners and centers; Florentinesque ornamentation is here transformed into bizarre linear forms. Mid-17th century. *Vienna, Kunsthistorisches Museum.*

141 Spanish plate frame with carved ornaments. Small format. Mid-17th century. *London, National Gallery.*

142 Spanish plate frame. The ornaments in ochre, white, light blue, and red on blue ground. Second half of the 18th century. *Berlin, Lemke.*

Spanish, Portuguese, and Latin American Frames

143 Spanish plate frame. Silver casing heightened with gold with dark blue and red ornamentation. Second half of the 18th century. *Berlin, Lemke.*

144 Spanish plate frame. The plate surface with engraved leafwork; carved ornamentation in the corners and center areas. (The center ornament of the horizontal molding has been obscured by shortening; cf. the form of the blossoms in the vertical members). Second half of the 17th century. *London, National Gallery.*

145 Spanish plate frame. The outer edge slanted outward. The smooth surfaces between the ornaments are in silver, the ornaments themselves are gilt; mid-17th century. *Oxford, Ashmolean Museum.*

Spanish, Portuguese, and Latin American Frames

146 Spanish plate frame with box-like, heightened border. The plate fishscale-like with rosettes in the centers and corners alternating with carved diamond shapes. Gilt throughout. Early 17th century. *Munich, Bayerische Staatsgemäldesammlungen.*

147 Detail of the carving of a leafwork frame of Spanish or Neapolitan origin. The laurel rod is arranged in fishscale-like manner; the leaf ornaments and the depressed tongue-like pattern is achieved by deep cuts. 17th century. *Munich, Bayerische Staatsgemäldesammlungen.*

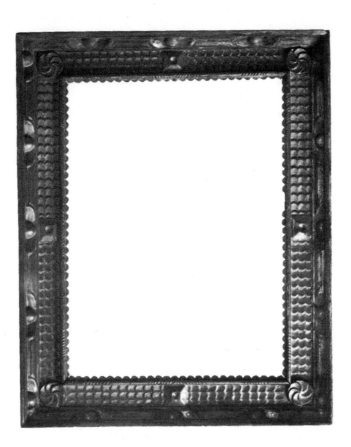

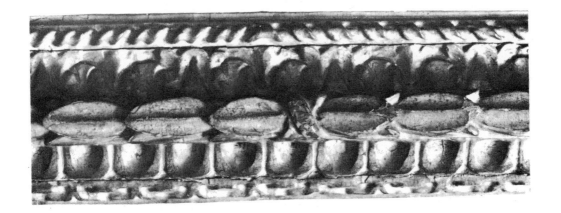

Spanish, Portuguese, and Latin American Frames

148 Peruvian plate frame, gilded with fishscale-like pattern, rosettes, and concave exterior border. 17th century. *Cuzco, Museo Historico Regional.*

149 Plate frame of Spanish or Neapolitan origin. The inner edge is accentuated by a laurel rod. On the plate are large acanthus leaves. 17th century. *Munich, Bayerische Gemäldesammlungen.*

150 Leaf frame, gilded. Bolivia, c.1700. *La Paz, Banco Central de Bolivia.*

151 Plate frame with cassette pattern. In the centers of the cassettes are placed small stone color disks, surrounded by rings. Cuzco School; Peru, early 17th century. *New Orleans Museum of Art.*

152 Portuguese profile frame, gilded. On the ribbed, half-round main profile fishscale-like rows of leaves alternate with scrollwork cartouches. 17th century. *Munich, Riggauer.*

153 Portuguese plate frame, gilded. Mid-17th century. *Berlin, Lemke.*

154 Detail of no. 152.

Netherlandish, Flemish, and Alpine Frames

155 Dutch channel frame with ebony veneer. Mid-17th century. *Munich, Bayerische Staatsgemäldesammlungen.*

156 Octagonal Dutch ebony frame combining channels and plate surfaces divided by a superimposed, ribbed profile. The painting was probably not in this frame originally. Mid-17th century. *Rotterdam, Museum Boymans-van Beuningen.*

157 Dutch frame with flat, stained strips of wood. Originally not intended for this picture. Mid-17th century. *Munich, Bayerische Staatsgemäldesammlungen.*

158 Dutch plate frame with figural carvings, corner medallions, and a cartouche in the lower border. It is the original frame for the portrait of the poet Jacob Cats (1577-1660), painted by Michiel van Miereveldt (1567-1641). *Amsterdam, Rijksmuseum.*

Netherlandish, Flemish, and Alpine Frames

159 Ornamental frame in small format (exterior height 21 cm), originally used for the miniature portrait of the painter Moses Terborch (1645-1647), painted by Gerard Terborch (1617-1681), c.1662. *Holland, Private Collection.*

160 Dutch leafwork and scrollwork frame, gilded, for a portrait of Abraham van Blijenberch, c.1602. *London, Christie's Sale,* 27 May 1977.

161   Octagonal Dutch frame of whalebone, polished and blackened. Originally made for the portrait of
the wife of an Amsterdam (?) painter, dated 1645. *Amsterdam, Rijksmuseum.*

Netherlandish, Flemish, and Alpine Frames

162 Flemish plate frame with black verneer and inlaid ivory rods. The picture did not belong to this frame originally. c.1600. *Munich, Bayerische Staatsgemäldesammlungen.*

163 Tortoise shell frame, presumably from southern Germany. The tortoise shell is laid on a gilt base. The picture did not belong to the frame originally. c.1600. *Munich, Bayerische Staatsgemäldesammlungen.*

164 Tortoise shell frame from Southern Germany or Austria. The plate is covered with ebony veneer with silver ornaments nailed on, which surround brownish sections of tortoise shell. Under the veneer, the base is painted red to heighten the effect of the tortoise shell. The latter is bevelled, diminishing in thickness toward the inner edge. The outer flame-like molding is of ebony. Early 17th century. *Munich, Bayerische Staatsgemäldesammlungen.*

165 Alpine frame without veneer. Mid-17th century. *Munich, Pfefferle.*

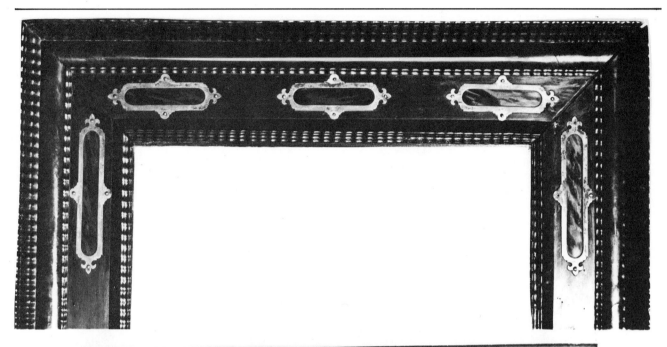

Netherlandish, Flemish, and Alpine Frames

166 Memorial tablet for Antistes Johann Jakob Breitinger of Zurich. Scrollwork frame with black veneer, framing a combination of portrait medallions and a stone tablet. Zurich 1635. *Zurich, Schweizerisches Landesmuseum.*

167   Detail of a "Flame-Molding" frame, Alpine or southern German variation. Mid-17th century.

168   Popular profile frame with superimposed flame molding and rosettes. Presumably Tyrolean; 17th century.
      Munich, Private Collection.

Netherlandish, Flemish, and Alpine Frames

169 Molding frame from southern Germany with extended octagonal corners ("ears"). The edges are smooth, and the convex surfaces shallow. Not intended for the picture presently in this frame. Early 17th century. *Munich, Bayerische Staatsgemäldesammlungen.*

170   Molding frame from Southern Germany with extended, octagonal, trimmed corners. Early 17th century.
      Munich, Riggauer.

Netherlandish, Flemish, and Alpine Frames

171 Dutch ivory frame, reminiscent of old-Netherlandish channel frames. The illusionistic device of the sitter's hand extended on the frame continues an invention of Hans Memling (cf. nos. 47-49). The frame, here illustrated, was lost during World War II. It housed the (self-?) portrait of Pieter Nason (c.1612-1688/90). *Warsaw, National Museum.*

172-76 Examples of picturesque use of flame moldings in southern German and Alpine frames of the mid-17th century.

172 *Munich, Riggauer.*

Netherlandish, Flemish, and Alpine Frames

173 *Munich, Pfefferle.*

174 *Munich, Pfefferle.*

175   *Munich, Pfefferle.*

176   (the picture did not belong to the frame originally)   *Amsterdam, Rijksmuseum.*

177   Lutma frame, named after the Dutch goldsmith and engraver, Jan Lutma the Younger (1624-1685) with representations of trophies of war and cornucopeia, as harbinger of peace. Originally housed "The Apotheosis of Cornelis de Witt," painted by Jan de Baen (1653-1702), c.1670. *Amsterdam, Rijksmuseum.*

178   Detail of a carved frame with heads of putti (horizontal members) and floral arrangements (vertical members). Originally made to house a portrait of Maria Henrietta Stuart (1631-1660), painted by Bartholomaeus van der Helst (1613-1670), dated 1652. *Amsterdam, Rijksmuseum.*

179   Overabundant Lutma frame made for the "Feast of St. Nicolaus," painted c.1660/70 by Jan Steen (1620-1679). *Amsterdam, Rijksmuseum.*

180   Lower border of a Lutma frame, mid-17th century. *Munich, Bayerische Staatsgemäldesammlungen.*

181   Lutma frame, made for the portrait of a sea captain, dated 1667, by Ferdinand Bol (1616-1680). *Amsterdam, Rijksmuseum.*

Netherlandish, Flemish, and Alpine Frames

182   Lutma frame for the "Self-Portrait" of c.1660 by Ferdinand Bol (1616-1680). *Amsterdam, Rijksmuseum.*

183   Example of a scenic semi-relief carving of a late Mannerist frame outside of Holland, perhaps Venetian, with the representation of a battle scene. Presumably intended originally for the portrait of a commander or an allegory. Mid-17th century. *Amsterdam, Rijksmuseum.*

184 Lutma frame of small format with floral and fruit decoration, made for a family portrait by Jan Mytens (1614-1670). Mid-17th century. *Groningen, Groninger Museeum voor stad en lande.*

185 Detail of the corner of a Lutma frame with hanging and intertwined blossoming vines; 1660/70. *Munich, Bayerische Staatsgemäldesammlungen.*

186 Lutma frame. The decorations are extended upward, so that they seem to be suspended from the corner; c.1660. *Amsterdam, Rijksmuseum.*

187   Lutma frame; presumably made for a portrait. It demonstrates the transition from scrollwork to foliage
      ornamentation; c.1670. *Amsterdam, Rijksmuseum.*

188   Gilded bronze frame with heads of putti in the manner of Alessandro Algardi (1602-1654). The silver bees are placed on the lapis lazuli ground of the escutcheon of the Barberini family, surrounded by a wreath of silver foliage. Rome, mid-17th century. *London, Private Collection.*

Sculptured Frames

189 Carved Italian frame with sumptuous foliage and floral ornamentation, including putti and symbols of the Passion. The painting of the Madonna is of a later date. Last third of the 17th century. *Munich, Bayerische Staatsgemäldesammlungen.*

190   Carved Italian frame, probably provincial. Closely akin in style to Bolognese frames; c.1600. *Milan, Museo Poldi Pezzoli.*

191   Luxury frame in the Venetian style with angels, sphinxes, dolphins, and the crest of the Bourbons. The painting did not belong to the frame originally. c.1600. *London, Christie's Sale* 9 July 1976.

Italian Baroque Frames

192   Plate frame with semi-relief vine ornamentation bordered on the inside by thick convex leafwork, and on the outside by tongue-shaped decoration. Second half of the 17th century. *Munich, Private Collection.*

193   Leaf frame, decreasing in thickness in steps toward the outside. The channel is decorated by superimposed acanthus leaves; c.1600. *Munich, Bayerische Staatsgemäldesammlungen.*

194   Leaf frame with a broad band of acanthus leaves. First half of the 17th century. *Munich, Bayerische Staatsgemäldesammlungen.*

195   Bolognese leafwork frame with putti. c.1680/90. *Venice, Museo Correr.*

196 Leaf frame with sumptuous tracery of acanthus leaves. The even symmetrical arrangement of the ornamentation is partly interrupted. Bologna, c.1660/70. *London, National Gallery.*

197 Leafwork frame with bunches of acanthus protruding. Bologna, 1680/90. *Hanover, Niedersächsische Landesgalerie.*

198   Circular leaf frame, interrupted by vines. Bologna, 1660/70. *Bologna, Pinacoteca Nazionale.*

199   Leaf frame consisting of a convex inner border of acanthus leaves, and an outer frame of perforated, evenly scrolled acanthus vines. Bologna, 1650/60. *Munich, Bayerische Staatsgemäldesammlungen.*

200 "Maratta Frame," gilded. Made for the portrait of Cardinal Jacopo Rospigliosi (1628-1713), painted by Carlo Maratta (1626-1713) between 1667 and 1669. *Cambridge, Fitzwilliams Museum.*

201 Detail of no. 200.

202 Neapolitan molding frame with an inner border of a gilded leaf rod, the remainder stained in a dark color. Wide channel divided by a space from a round rod. Early 18th century. *Munich, Bayerische Staatsgemälde-sammlungen.*

203 Neapolitan molding frame, stained in a dark color, consisting of a leaf rod and a pearl rod. Early 18th century.
Munich, Bayerische Staatsgemäldesammlungen.

204   Roman molding frame, so-called "Salvator Rosa Frame." Matte gilded with polished quarter-round channel
rod. Made for "Emperor Theodosius before St. Ambrosius," dated 1745, painted by Pierre Subleyras (1699-
1749). *Munich, Bayerische Staatsgemäldesammlungen.*

205 Roman "Salvator Rosa Frame" made for a representation of an Evangelist, painted by Pompeo Batoni (1708-1787), mid-18th century. *London, P. and D. Colnaghi.*

206 Roman "Salvator Rosa Frame," mid-18th century. *Berlin-Dahlem, Gemäldegalerie.*

207 Roman "Salvator Rosa Frame." Made for "Glorification of the Madonna and Child," painted in 1747 by Pompeo Batoni (1708-1787). *London, Speelman.*

208 Florentine leaf frame with abstract tongue and seashell ornamentation. c.1640/50. *Florence, Palazzo Pitti.*

209   Florentine leaf frame with tongue and ear lobe ornamentation. The plate of the frame is composed of several intertwined and perforated layers. Mid-17th century. *Florence, Palazzo Pitti.*

210   Florentine octagonal luxury frame of ebony with gilded bronze ornaments; ascribed to Giovanni Battista
      Foggini (1652-1725). Made for "Madonna and Child" by Carlo Dolci (1616-1686) in c.1697. *Florence,
      Palazzo Pitti.*

211   Vine frame, perhaps intended for a mirror, composed of enlarged acanthus leaves. Florence, c.1680.
Florence, Palazzo Pitti.

Italian Baroque Frames

212 Baguette-shaped leaf frame of a single convex laurel band tied with ribbons. The corners and centers are emphasized by protruding laurel. Italian, 17th century. *Munich, Bayerische Staatsgemäldesammlungen.*

213 Early example of stencilled ornamentation: Italian plate frame, with black edges and gilt ornamentation. 17th century. *Munich, Bayerische Staatsgemäldesammlungen.*

214   Stucco frame, detail. The stucco ornaments are here superimposed on a wood base. Gilt on thin chalk base. Polished areas alternate with the raised ornaments. Neapolitan (?), 18th century. *Munich, Bayerische Staatsgemäldesammlungen.*

215   "Canaletto Frame." Venetian molding frame with carved ornaments interrupted by "mirrors." Four dowels on the upper corners indicate that an additional piece, now lost, could be attached. Early 19th century. *Munich, Bayerische Staatsgemäldesammlungen.*

Italian Baroque Frames

216 Venetian Rococo frame with perforated, cartilage-like members. Gilt on red base. c.1750. *Munich, Riggauer.*

217 Venetian (?) profile frame of the time of Louis XIV. Cartouches are attached to protrude laterally; the ornamentation consists of alternating shield and seashell-shaped leaves; c.1700. *Munich, Bayerische Staatsgemäldesammlungen.*

218 Venetian leaf frame with shallow convex profile of densely curved laurel leaves and stylized fruit; gilded; dotted in the corners. Second half of the 17th century. *Munich, Bayerische Staatsgemäldesammlungen.*

Italian Baroque Frames

219   Venetian Rococo frame with interrupted cartilage-like ornamentation. It is not certain whether it was intended originally for the stylistically corresponding "St. Hyacinth" by Francesco Guardi (1712-1793) which it houses today. c.1750. *Vienna, Kunsthistorisches Museum.*

220   Venetian molding frame. The convex center is black with painted ornaments in reddish gold. This type of *chinoiserie* frame imitates East Asian lacquer work. Uncertain whether intended for a painting or a mirror. Mid-18th century. *Munich, Bayerische Staatsgemäldesammlungen.*

221   Venetian molding frame. The convex center is interrupted by engraved and gilded center and corner
decoration. The mirrors between them are silverplated and heightened with lacquer. Second half
of the 18th century. *Munich, Bayerische Staatsgemäldesammlungen.*

222   Venetian molding frame. The inner edge is decorated with leaves which seem as if folded over. The outside
edge consists of a round and a turned rod. Made for "Card Game." Painted c.1760 by Pietro Longhi (1702-
1785). *Munich, Bayerische Staatsgemäldesammlungen.*

223 Rococo frame, combining convex emphasis with undulating rocaille. It is not certain whether this frame was originally intended for the painting it now houses, "The Adoration" by Corrado Giaquinto (1703-1765). Italian, c.1750. *Vienna, Kunsthistorisches Museum.*

224 Venetian marbelized molding frame, with gilded ornaments. Mid-18th century. *Berlin, Lemke.*

225 Spanish molding frame, gilded and engraved, intended for a painting or a mirror (as suggested by the mirrored sections). Mid-18th century. *Berlin, Lemke.*

226 Spanish molding frame. Mid-18th century. *Berlin, Lemke.*

227 Plate frame painted black with gilded oblique inner edge and brass fittings. It belongs to a series of frames made for portraits of scholars. The sitter is John Tradescant the Elder (d. 1638), painted by Thomas (?) Decritz (c.1605-c.1676). It represents an ornamental form later taken over by Lutma and Gibbons. Mid-17th century. *Oxford, Ashmolean Museum.*

228   Ornamental frame of small format in the manner of Grinling Gibbons (1648-1721) with floral and blossom carvings. Made for a portrait of Queen Mary (1689-1694). c.1690. *London, Victoria and Albert Museum.*

229   Luxury frame in the manner of Grinling Gibbons (1648-1721). c.1690. *London, Victoria and Albert Museum.*

230 Carved frame made by Grinling Gibbons (1648-1721) for a portrait of King James II (1685-1688), painted by John Riley, c.1685. *Oxford, Ashmolean Museum.*

231   Large leaf frame with broad oak leaf-like ornamentation, surrounding an inner border of laurel. Originally made for a portrait of King James I, painted by Daniel Mytens (1590-1648), dated 1621. *London, National Portrait Gallery.*

Seventeenth Century English Frames

232 Corner of a "Lely Frame," named after Sir Peter Lely (1618-1680), wood, silvered, dating from c.1675, i.e. conforming to the series of frames made for the gallery of King Charles II at Windsor. *London, National Gallery.*

233 Corner of an English frame in the Lutma style with sumptuous carving of blossom and fruit, 1660/70. *Oxford, Ashmolean Museum.*

234 Detail of a bottom molding, English. Mid-17th century. *Munich, Bayerische Staatsgemäldesammlungen.*

235   "Sunderland Frame," the English variety of the "Lutma Frame." The soft, cartilage-like ear lobe structure
has here been transformed into a flat, draughtsman-like sweeping motion, conforming remarkably well with
the hairstyle and fashion of the time, although this frame did not house originally the present portrait of
Lord Thomas Clifford, painted by Lely about 1672. The frame was made between 1670 and 1675.
London, National Portrait Gallery.

236 English frame with ornamentation in the style of Louis XIII. Second half of the 17th century. *Copenhagen, Staatens Museum for Kunst.*

237 English frame in the style of Louis XIII. Second half of the 17th century. *London, Pollak.*

238 English frame in the style of Louis XIII, silvered. Probably made for the portrait of Samuel Pepys (1633-1703) painted by John Hayls, dated 1666. According to Pepys' diary, he paid £14 for the portrait and £25 for the frame. *London, National Portrait Gallery.*

239 Oval frame in the English Louis XIII/IV style. c.1700. *Munich, Riggauer.*

240 Corner of an English frame in the style of Louis XIII. Made for the portrait of the architect Christopher Wren (1632-1723), painted by Godfrey Kneller (1646-1723), dated 1712. *London, National Portrait Gallery.*

241 Corner of an English frame transitionary from the style of Louis XIII to that of Louis XIV. c.1700. *London, National Portrait Gallery.*

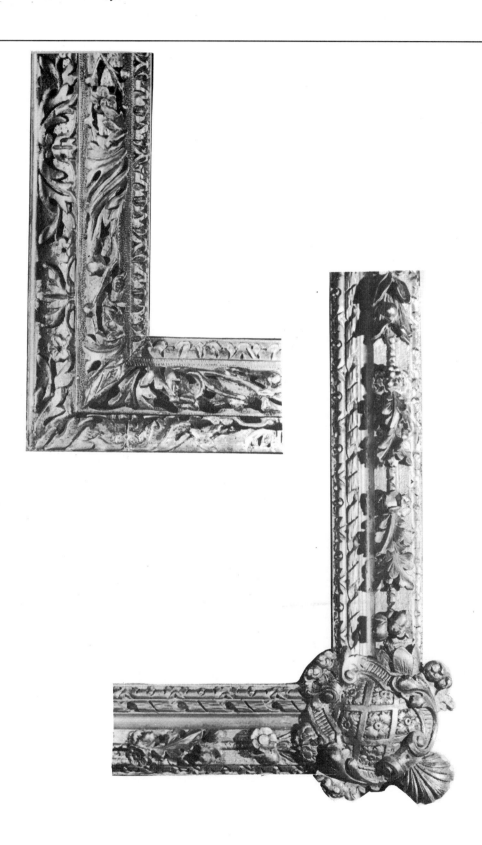

242 Wooden frame with flame molding along the edges and silver fittings mounted on the plate. South Germany, 17th century. *Munich, Riggauer.*

243 Profile frame made of wood with tortoiseshell inlays, made to house a representation of Banda Neira, Indonesia. Made in the Netherlands or East India. c.1700. *Amsterdam, Rijksmuseum.*

Various Materials

244 Wooden frame with frieze-like silver foil superimposed, inlaid with semiprecious stones and cast bronze corners. Italy, second half of the 16th century. *Paris, Lebrun.*

245 Silver frame (height 31 cm) for a portrait of Louis XIV. Parisian imprint of 1672/73. *London, Victoria and Albert Museum.*

Various Materials

246   Cast iron frame for a miniature or plaque. The plate is cut and forged. 17th century. *Rouen, Musée Secq des Tournelles.*

247   Ceramic frame, kiln-baked and glazed. South German or Austrian, 1775-80. *Munich, Private Collection.*

248   Detail of no. 247.

249   Cast iron frame for a miniature or plaquette. 17th century. *Rouen, Musée Secq des Tournelles.*

250 Wooden frame with pietra-dura inlays and painted ornamentation. French "Adikur Frame." Late 16th century.
Oxford, Ashmolean Museum.

251 Small frame made of brass plate, embossed and silver plated. Presumably intended for a devotional picture. South German, c.1790. *Munich, Riggauer.*

French Frames

252 "Clouet Frame" with pietra-dura inlay and painted ornamentation. Mid-16th century. *London, National Gallery.*

253 Altar frame, donated by the Confrérie du Puits Notre Dame d'Amiens, 1525. *Amiens, Musée de Picardie.*

254   Altar frame, donated by the Confrérie du Puits Notre Dame d'Amiens, 1518. *Amiens, Musée de Picardie.*

255   Louis XIII frame with dense aggregate of profiles. Mid-18th century. *Paris, Lebrun.*

French Frames

256   Louis XIII frame with geometrical ornamentation, anticipating the style of Louis XIV. Mid-17th century. *Paris, Musée des Arts Decoratifs.*

257   Louis XIII frame. Mid-17th century. *Paris, Lebrun.*

258   Louis XIII frame. Mid-17th century. *Paris, Musée des Arts Decoratifs.*

259   Transitional frame type to the style of Louis XIV; plastic individualization of the ornaments. The appearance of the frame is hampered by the lack of gilding. Second half of the 17th century. *Paris, Musée des Arts Decoratifs.*

260   Louis XIII frame. Mid-17th century. *Paris, Cailleux.*

French Frames

261   Early Louis XIV frame. Second half of the 17th century. *Paris, Lebrun.*

262   Louis XIV frame with alternating sections of smooth surfaces ("mirrors") and carved blossom and leafwork decoration. c.1690. *Paris, Cailleux.*

263   Oval Louis XIV frame of the same time as no. 262. *Paris, Musée des Arts Décoratifs.*

264 Louis XIV frame of the same time as no. 262. The surfaces are decorated with engraved blossom ornaments which have their origin in the style of Louis XIII. c.1690. *Munich, Pfefferle.*

265 Early Louis XV frame with the Bourbon crest. Paris, c.1735. *Paris, Cailleux.*

266 "Regency Frame" with oval cut-out. c.1730. *Paris, Cailleux.*

267   Detail of late Louis XIV frame. Paris 1715/20. *Munich, Bayerische Staatsgemäldesammlungen.*

268   Late Louis XIV frame, not intended for the picture it now houses. 1715/20. *Oxford, Ashmolean Museum.*

269 Louis XIV frame. Ca. 1710. *Paris, Musée des Arts Décoratifs*

French Frames

270 Detail of no. 271.

271 Late Louis XIV frame; transitional to the Regency style. c.1720. *Paris, Cailleux.*

272   Regency Frame. c.1725/30. *Melbourne, National Gallery of Victoria.*

French Frames

273   Detail from no. 272.

274   Regency Frame. c.1725/30. *Berlin, Lemke.*

212

275   Regency Frame. c.1725. *Paris, Lebrun.*

276   Late Regency Frame with cut-out having a curved top. Entirely out of a single piece of wood. c.1730. *London, National Gallery.*

277   Early Louis XV frame in oblong format surmounted by a carved section. c.1735. *Paris, Musée des Arts Décoratifs.*

French Frames

278 Regency Frame. c.1730. *Paris, Musée des Arts Décoratifs.*

279 Louis XV frame with oval cut-out. c.1740. *London, Pollak.*

280   Regency Frame. c.1730. *Melbourne, National Gallery of Victoria.*

281   Detail from no. 280.

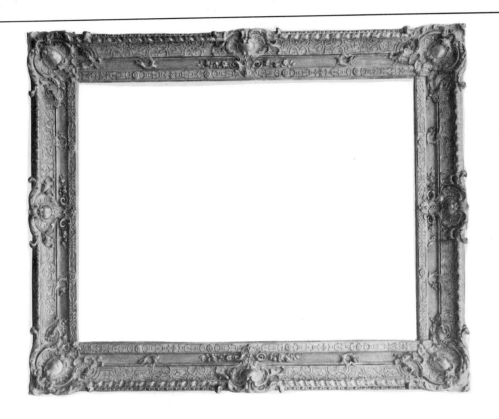

French Frames

282   Regency Frame. French provincial; probably from southern France. c.1725/30. *Paris, Lebrun.*

283   Frame type exemplifying the transition to the style of Louis XV. c.1735. *Paris, Cailleux.*

284 Detail from no. 285.

285 Louis XV frame. Paris, c.1740. *Munich, Bayerische Staatsgemaldesammlungen.*

286 Detail from no. 285.

287   Louis XV Luxury frame (470 x 320 cm) with the coat of arms of Lorraine. Nancy, dated 1740. *Paris, Musée des Arts Décoratifs.*

288 Louis XV frame with oval cut-out. c.1740/50. *Paris, Musée des Arts Décoratifs.*

289 Oval Louis XV frame. c.1740/50. *Paris, Musée des Arts Décoratifs.*

290 Oblong oval Louis XV frame, not intended for the picture it now houses. c.1740/50. *Paris, Cailleux.*

291 Transitional frame to the style of Louis XVI. The outer contours are clearly defined and the overall appearance, as well as the ornamentation is geometrical. The frame is surmounted by the crest of Mme. de Pompadour (1721-1764). Small cuts are evidence of a reduction of the format. c.1755. *Versailles, Musée Nationale de Versailles.*

292   Late Louis XV frame. The flat surfaces have been dissolved into a flowing frame zone, varying in width. Between 1745 and 1750. *Paris, Cailleux.*

French Frames

295   Transitional frame; not intended for the picture it now houses. c.1755. *Paris, Cailleux.*

296   Fragment of the upper edge of a Louis XVI frame. c.1770. *Paris, Musée des Arts Décoratifs.*

French Frames

297   Louis XVI frame. Between 1770 and 1780. *Paris, Musée des Arts Décoratifs.*

298   Louis XVI frame, signed *Etienne Louis Infroit,* made to house the still-life painted by Henri Horace Roland de la Porte (1724-93) which was exhibited at the Salon of 1769. *Private Collection.*

299   Detail of no. 298, showing the signature on the verso.

300 Louis XVI frame, not intended for the picture it now houses. Between 1770 and 1780. *Paris, Cailleux.*

301 Louis XVI frame. Between 1770 and 1780. *Paris, Musée des Arts Décoratifs.*

302 Louis XVI frame with oval cut-out. c.1780. *Paris, Musée des Arts Décoratifs.*

303 Louis XVI frame with the Bourbon coat of arms. Between 1770 and 1780. *Paris, Cailleux.*

304   Louis XVI frame (not made for the portrait it now houses). Signed on the verso: *C. Infroit* (Claude Infroit, the son of Etienne Louis Infroit). Last quarter of the 18th century. *Waddesdon Manor, National Trust.*

French Frames

305   Louis XVI frame. Signed on the verso: *T. Dumont* (Thomas Dumont from Nancy, c.1755–after 1792). Made for the portrait of a lady it still houses. c.1780. *Waddesdon Manor, National Trust.*

306   Detail of the signature on the verso of no. 304.

228

307 Louis XVI frame, made for the portrait of the Marquis de St. Paul, painted by Jean Baptiste Greuze (1725-1805), dated 1760. The frame is signed *A. Levert. Amsterdam, Rijksmuseum.*

308 Oval Louis XVI frame. c.1780. *Paris, Lebrun.*

309   Louis XVI frame. c.1790. *Paris, Musée des Arts Décoratifs.*

310   Louis XVI frame made for the portrait of Anne Vallayer-Coster (1744-1818), exhibited at the Salon of 1783 with a similarly framed companion piece. *Private Collection.*

311 Louis XVI frame. Between 1770 and 1780. *Paris, Lebrun.*

312 Oval Louis XVI frame, probably made for a different picture than it houses today. Between 1770 and 1780. *Paris, Cailleux.*

313   Detail of no. 312.

314   Louis XVI frame. Between 1780 and 1790. *Paris, Musée des Arts Décoratifs.*

315 Louis XVI frame; probably made in Germany, for the portrait in pastel of Princess Augusta Dorothea
of Brunswick (1789-1830) painted by Johann Heinrich Schroeder (1757-1812) between 1775 and 1780.
Weimar, Ducal Palace.

Eighteenth Century English Frames

316 Leaf frame, freely based on models of ornamentation in the style of Louis XIV. In this example (cf. no. 196), the carved leafwork is concentrated in the main portion of the frame, similar to Italian examples (cf. nos. 196, 198, 199). The outer moldings are ornamented in typically Louis XIV fashion. This large frame was probably made for the portrait of Sir Isaac Newton (1643-1727), painted in 1702 by Geoffrey Kneller (1646-1723). *London, National Portrait Gallery.*

317 Profile frame with rocaille ornamentation in the style of Louis XV. c.1750. *London, Pollak.*

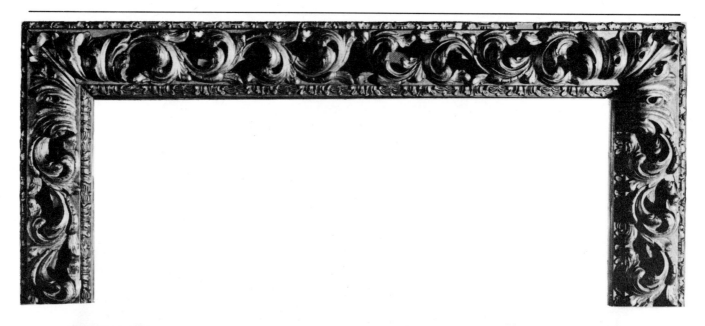

318   George I, Regency Frame. c.1720. *London, Pollak.*

Eighteenth Century English Frames

319　Luxury frame in the style of Louis XV (George II), made for a portrait in 1756 by Thomas Hudson (1701-1779). *London, Sale Christie's,* 7 July 1967.

320　Sumptuous Louis XV (George II) frame attributed to Thomas Chippendale (1709-1779), made for the portrait of the Prince of Wales (1738-1820), later George III (crowned 1760). c.1755. *London, Victoria and Albert Museum.*

321　Late Rococo (George I–George II) frame, housing a portrait of the Countess of Winchester, painted by Geoffrey Kneller (1646-1723) between 1776 and 1784. The frame may have been made about twenty years earlier. *Ditchley Park, Oxfordshire.*

322   Louis XV (George II) frame of small format. c.1755/60. *London, Pollak.*

323   Lateral portion of a large transitional frame (George III), measuring 145 cm in height), not made for the picture it now houses. c.1765. *London, National Gallery.*

324 Louis XV (George II) frame. c.1760. *London, Pollak.*

325 Finial of a Louis XVI (George III) frame, made for a portrait of Mrs. Delany (1700-1788), painted by John Opie (1761-1807), between 1780 and 1785. *London, National Portrait Gallery.*

326   English "Maratta Frame." Made for the self-portrait of Thomas Gainsborough (1727-1788), painted in 1787. *London, Royal Academy.*

327   English "Maratta Frame," last quarter of the 18th century. *London, Pollak.*

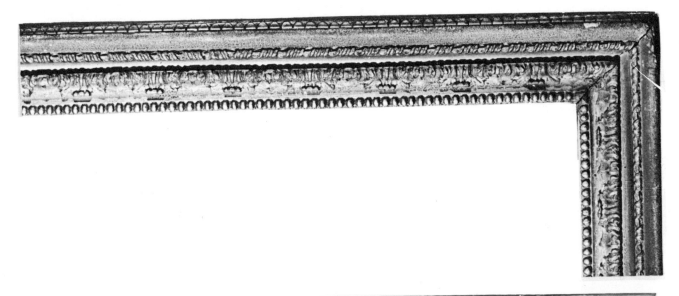

328   Early neoclassical frame. Last quarter of the 18th century. *London, Pollak.*

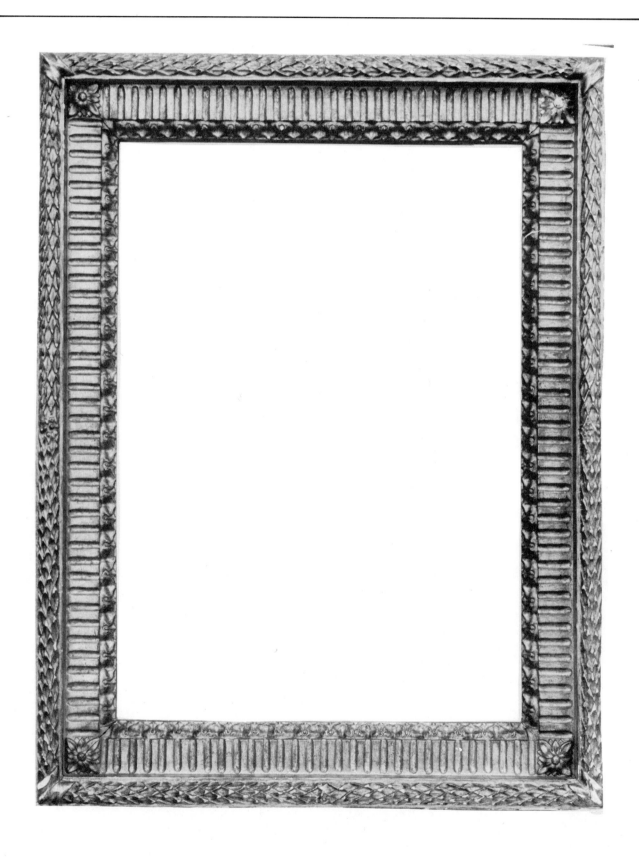

329   Wooden model for a goldsmith, made for the devotional image of Sonntagbert (Lower Austria), made by
Melchior Hefele (1716-1799) in 1751. *Berlin-Charlottenburg, Kunstgewerbemuseum.*

Late Baroque Frames in Other Countries

330 Corner ornament of the frame of an auxiliary altarpiece in the convent church of Kremsmünster (Upper Austria). c.1700.

331 Corner of an Austrian Regency frame. Between 1720 and 1730. *Munich, Riggauer.*

332 Corner of an Austrian frame, transitional from Regency to Rococo. c.1735. *Munich, Riggauer.*

333 Corner of an Austrian Rococo (Louis XV) frame, made between 1740 and 1750. *Munich, Riggauer.*

334 Carved frame of the late Louis XIV style. Made at the Saxonian Court. c.1720. *Formerly at Moritzburg Hunting Chalet. Saxony.*

335 Carved frame, transitional from Regency to Rococo. Berlin or Potsdam, between 1735 and 1740. *Munich, Riggauer.*

336 Carved Rococo frame with the coat of arms of Bishop Johann Philipp von Greiffenklau of Würzburg (1749-1754). Not made for the picture it now houses. c.1750 (damaged on all sides). *Munich, Bayerische Staatsgemäldesammlungen.*

337 Detail of the partially damaged ornamentation of no. 336.

338-340   Frames made at the Prussian Court. Potsdam-Berlin, c.1750. *Berlin-Charlottenburg Palace.*

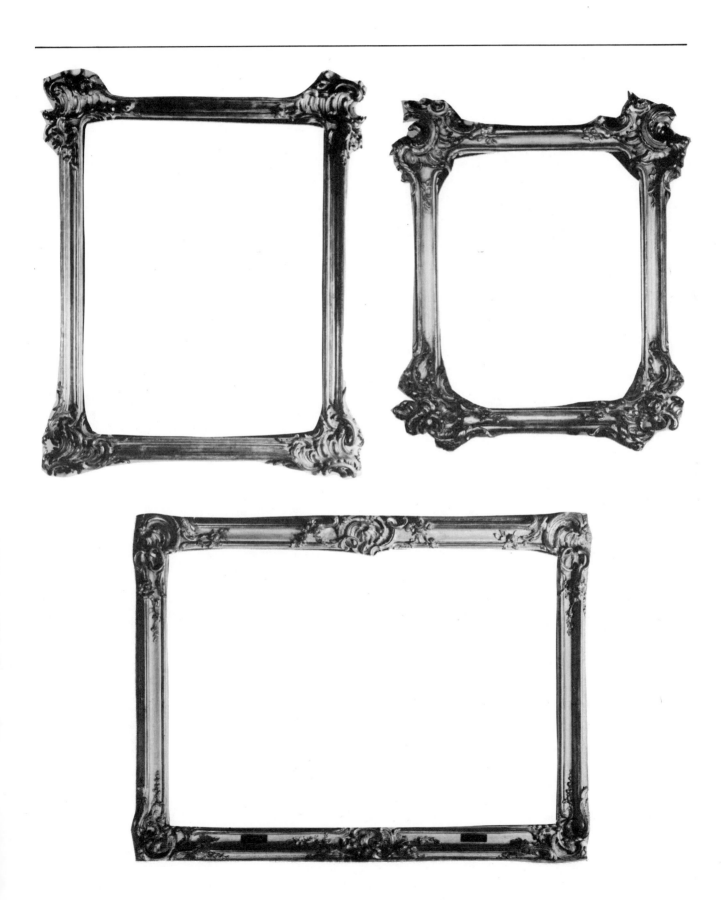

Late Baroque Frames in Other Countries

341 Carved Rococo frame, made for the double-portrait of the Court Jeweler Fabritius and his wife, painted by Peder Als (1726-1776). Danish, c.1760. *Copenhagen, Statens Museum for Kunst.*

342 Carved Rococo frame, made for a portrait of a lady, painted by Georg Desmarées (1697-1776). One of a series of frames made for an Upper Bavarian Chateau. Bavarian, c.1760. *Munich, Private Collection.*

343 Carved Rococo frame. Probably not made for the picture it now houses. Danish, c.1760. *Copenhagen, Statens Museum for Kunst.*

Late Baroque Frames in Other Countries

344 Late Baroque carved frame from northern Russia. Gilded linden wood. On the flat plate, carved acanthus vines, arranged around curved branches, have been placed, akin to Italian models of the late 17th century. Probably mid-18th century, made in connection with the Italianate Russian Rastreli style. *Private Collection.*

345 Detail from no. 344.

346   Rococo frame of small format. South German, made between 1750 and 1760. *Munich, Fischer-Böhler.*

347   Early neoclassical frame with the crest of Pope Pius VII, housing a mosaic by Filippo Cocchi (?). Rome, dated 1785. *Copenhagen, Kunstindustriemuseet.*

348   Louis XVI frame, made for the portrait of the Elector Frederick Augustus of Saxony (1750-1827) in 1791, painted by Anton Graff (1736-1813). *London, Private Collection.*

349   Early neoclassical frame for the double-portrait of Emperor Joseph II (1741-1790) and of his brother Leopold (1747-1792), painted in 1769 by Pompeo Batoni (1708-1787). *Vienna, Kunsthistorisches Museum.*

350   Early neoclassical frame of gilded bronze with lapis lazuli inlay, cast in the workshop of the Vatican, Rome, c.1775. It frames a mosaic copy of the portrait no. 349. *Vienna, Kunsthistorisches Museum.*

351   Carved corner ornament on a neoclassical frame. Italian, early 19th century. *Rome, Pinacoteca Vaticana.*

Late Baroque Frames in Other Countries

352 Neoclassical molding frame from southern Germany. c.1800. *Munich, Riggauer.*

353 Neoclassical molding frame with a wide channel and "pipe" cut, framed by a convex laurel border. Rome, end of the 18th century. *Munich, Bayerische Staatsgemäldesammlungen.*

354 Neoclassical molding frame made for the double-portrait of the children of the artist Andrea Appiani (1754-1817). Milan, 1808. *Munich, Bayerische Staatsgemäldesammlungen.*

355 Neoclassical molding frame, covered with a strip of laurel leaves. Probably made for the portrait of Mme. de Prangin, painted by Jens Juel (1745-1802), dated 177[?]. *Copenhagen, Statens Museum for Kunst.*

Gallery Frames

356-62 "Effner" frames in the Regency style, made in the workshops of the electoral court in Munich for the palaces at Munich and Schleissheim. *Munich, Bayerische Staatsgemäldesammlungen.*

356 Simple, engraved frame, probably made for a less important private chamber in the Munich palace. c.1740.

357 Made for Schleissheim Palace with three-dimensional emblems in the center (not illustrated here), for Rubens' "Henry IV at the Battle of St. Martin d'Eglise." c.1725.

358, 359, 361 Made for the gallery in Schleissheim Palace between 1720 and 1725.

360, 362   Made for the palace in Munich. c.1730/35.

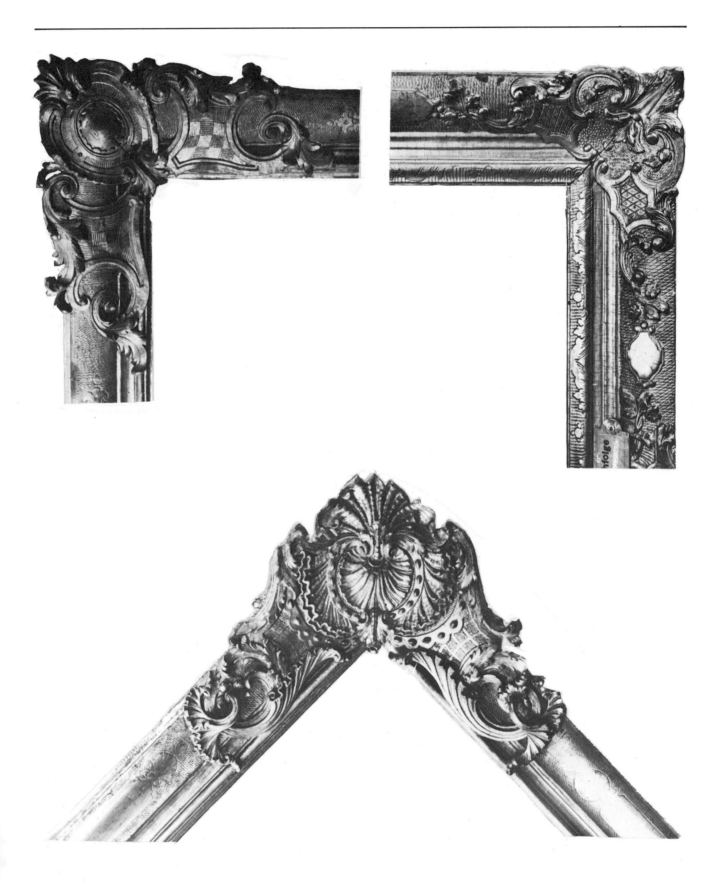

Gallery Frames

363   Rococo frame for the Dresden Gallery. c.1765. *Dresden, Staatliche Kunstsammlungen.*

364   Frame from the Düsseldorf Gallery in late Louis XIV style. c.1710. *Munich, Bayerische Staatsgemäldesammlungen.*

365 "Cuvilliés" frame. Louis XV frame made in the workshops of the court at Munich. c.1740. *Munich, Bayerische Staatsgemäldesammlungen.*

366 Detail of the corner of no. 363.

Gallery Frames

367 Rococo frame from the Dresden Gallery. c.1765. *Dresden, Staatliche Kunstsammlungen.*

368 "Pitti" frame. Florentine late Baroque, as found in many examples in Pitti Palace. Florence, end of the 17th century. *Florence, Palazzo Pitti.*

369 Frame from the Dresden Gallery with octagonal cut-out, made for "St. Cecilia" painted by Carlo Dolci (1616-1686). c.1765. *Dresden, Staatliche Kunstsammlungen.*

370 Neoclassical "Schinkel" frame, based on the designs of the architect Friedrich Schinkel (1781-1841), and used in the Berlin *Gemäldegalerie* as uniform standard frame, 1823-1830. *Berlin-Dahlem, Gemäldegalerie.*

Gallery Frames

371 "Klenze" frame with octagonal cut-out for the "Repentant Magdalen" by Carlo Dolci (1616-1686). Named for the Munich architect of the *Alte Pinakotek,* Leo von Klenze (1784-1864), who provided the design for the uniform frames of that museum, 1830-1836. *Munich, Bayerische Staatsgemäldesammlungen.*

372 Corner of a Munich gallery frame, transitional from Rococo to Louis XVI style, between 1765 and 1770. *Munich, Bayerische Staatsgemäldesammlungen.*

373 Corner of a gallery frame from the former gallery at Düsseldorf; early neoclassical, made between 1770 and 1775. *Munich, Bayerische Staatsgemäldesammlungen.*

374 Corner of an early neoclassical frame of the Munich Hofgarten Gallery. Made from designs of the Court Architect Karl Albert von Lespilliez (1723-1796) in c.1779. *Munich, Bayerische Staatsgemäldesammlungen.*

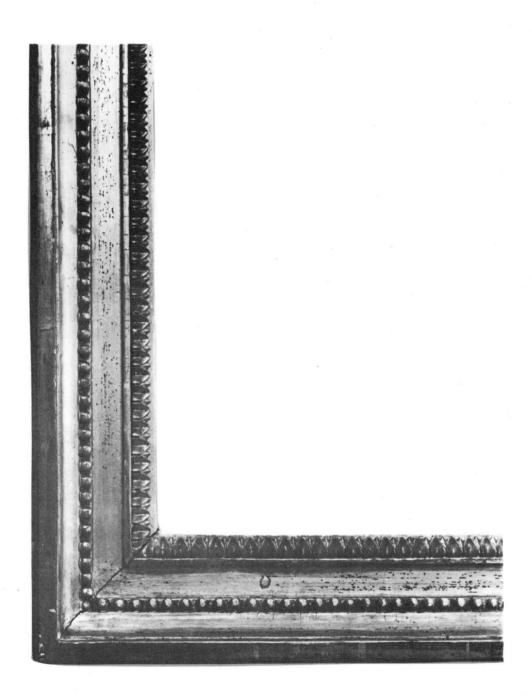

375 Neoclassicist frame, profusely carved and gilded. France, c.1800.

376 Detail of no. 375.

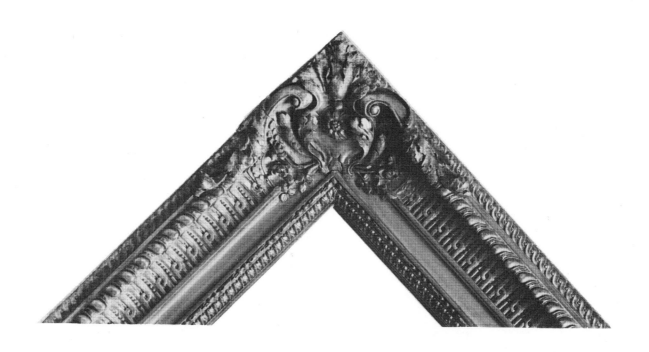

377 Corner of a carved wooden frame, based on the design of Jean Auguste Dominique Ingres (1780-1867). Paris, between 1840 and 1850. *New York, Metropolitan Museum of Art.*

378 Corner of a frame designed by Ingres for the portrait of Mme. Moitessier, dated 1856. The ornamentation is made from gilder's compound. Before the acquisition of the portrait, in 1936, the frame was ordered to be removed because the trustees thought it unsuitable. It was later reinstalled. *London, National Gallery.*

From Classicism to Historicism

379 Neoclassical molding frame with neo-Gothic, reinterpreted, pressed-on ornamentation. German, between 1810 and 1825. *Munich, Riggauer.*

380 Neoclassical molding frame. German, beginning of the 19th century. *Munich, Pfefferle.*

381   Neoclassical molding frame with palmettes. French or German, early 19th century. *Munich, Pfefferle.*

382   Neoclassical molding frame with pressed-on palmette and vine ornamentation. German, early 19th century. *Munich, Riggauer.*

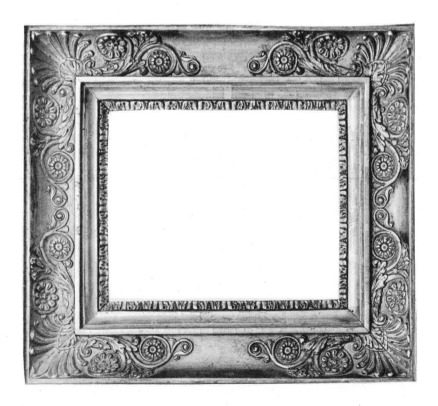

383   Neoclassical molding frame with pressed-on foliage and blossom ornamentation. *Munich, Private Collection.*

384   Neoclassical molding frame with foliage ornaments made of papier machée. *Munich, Riggauer.*

385 Neoclassical molding frame with carved attachments and sumptuous pressed-on ornaments. It probably housed the portrait of a child since inception. Southern German, c.1830. *Private Collection.*

386 Neoclassical molding with pressed-on palmette ornamentation, made of papier machée. England, early 19th century. *Oxford, Ashmolean Museum.*

387 Late classicizing luxury frame. Caste bronze, and electronically gold-plated unit, mounted on a wooden base. Made for a portrait in miniature on porcelain of King Frederick William IV of Prussia, after a design by Gustav Stier (1807-1880) between 1842 and 1844 in Berlin. *Berlin-Charlottenburg, Gewerbemuseum.*

388   Plate frame with painted ornamental band of vines and bell-shaped blossoms. Made for the portrait "Maler Hilker" by Christian Købke (1810-1848), c.1837. *Copenhagen, Statens Museum for Kunst.*

389   Gothicizing molding frame of the Romantic period. The vine ornamentation is drawn on the gilded base. Made for "Walk to Emmaus" by Joseph von Führich (1800-1876). Vienna, 1837. *Bremen, Kunsthalle.*

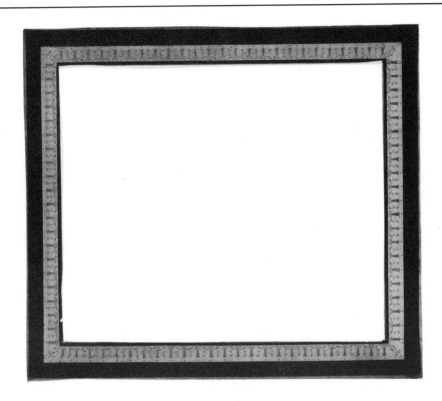

390   Neo-Baroque frame of the painting "The Haywagon" by John Constable (1776-1837), exhibited in London in 1821, and in Paris in 1824. Although called "original," the frame probably dates from about the middle of the century. *London, National Gallery.*

391   German Biedermeier frame with pressed-on rococo decorations. Made for "Heroic Landscape" by Johann Martin von Rohden (1778-1868), dated 1844. *Bremen, Kunsthalle.*

392   German Biedermeier frame with pressed-on flat rococo decoration. Made for "Blue Grotto" by Heinrich Jakob Fried (1802-1870), dated 1835. *Bremen, Kunsthalle.*

393   Frame designed by Dante Gabriel Rossetti (1828-1882) for his "Monna Pomona," dated 1864. *London, Tate Gallery.*

394   Frame designed by Dante Gabriel Rossetti for his "The Annunciation," dated 1850. *London, Tate Gallery.*

395   Frame designed by William Holman Hunt (1827-1910) for his "The Dovecoat," made in 1866, altered in 1875. *Oxford, Ashmolean Museum.*

396 Frame designed by John Everett Millais (1829-1896) for "Convent Thoughts," dated 1851, painted by Charles Allston Collins (1828-1873). The frame can be dated precisely because of a letter by Millais, dated 1 April 1851: "I have designed a frame for Charles' painting of lilies which I expect will be acknowledged to be the best frame in England." *Oxford, Ashmolean Museum.*

397 Frame for the portrait of Mrs. Alma-Tadema, painted in 1879 by Jules Bastien-Lepage (1848-1884). *Oxford, Ashmolean Museum.*

398 Frame designed and signed by James Abbott McNeill Whistler (1834-1903) with his butterfly emblem for "The White Girl," dated 1862. *Washington, National Gallery.*

399 Contemporary frame with engraved ornamentation and wide cuff, as inner border for "The Road to the Temple" by Lawrence Alma-Tadema (1836-1912), made in 1879. *London, Royal Academy.*

400 Frame for "There Sleeps Titania some Time of Night—Lull'd in these Flowers with Dances and Delight," painted by Robert Huskisson (d. 1854). The carved ornamentation is inspired by Sienese and Florentine models. *London, The Handley-Read Collection.*

401   Carved walnut frame by Luigi Frullini (1839-1897) with classicizing ornaments in the style of the early
      Renaissance: candelabra-like vertical, and arabesque-like horizontal arrangement of the carved decorations.
      Marked *Firenze 1872. Vienna, Oesterreichisches Museum für angewandte Kunst.*

402   Carved walnut frame by Francesco Morini, akin to no. 401. With emblems in the corners. Exhibited at the
      World Fair of 1873. Signed and dated *F. Morini Firenze 1872. Vienna, Oesterreiches Museum für angewandte
      Kunst.*

403   Carved walnut frame by Frullini or Morini (cf. nos. 401, 402). The vines with blossoms and animals, as well
      as the heads in the corners, were inspired by Lorenzo Ghiberti's (1381-1455) east portal of the Baptistry in
      Florence (1425-1452). Florence, c.1870. *Vienna, Oesterreisches Museum für angewandte Kunst.*

404   Carved frame for a painting on porcelain of the Berlin Porzellanmanufaktur, signed *Maliz;* last third of the 19th century. *New York, Sale Sotheby Parke-Bernet,* 17 January 1975.

405 Neoclassical frame with ribbed half-round columns and masks placed on the cube-like corners. Made for "Böcklin's Tomb," painted by Ferdinand Keller (1842-1922), c.1901/02. *Karlsruhe, Staatliche Kunsthalle.*

406 Neoclassical aedicula frame with raised half-round columns mounted on the flat frame plate, inscribed base, and ornamented architrave, made for "The Sin," painted by Franz von Stuck (1863-1928) in 1893. *Munich, Bayerische Staatsgemäldesammlungen.*

407   Art Nouveau frame of wood, covered with an embossed, silver-plated brass plate, made by Georg Klimt (b. 1867) for "Judith and Holofernes," painted by Gustav Klimt (1862-1918).   *Vienna, Oesterreichische Galerie.*

408 Plate frame with painted decorations by Gustav Klimt for his portrait of Josef Pembaur (1848-1923), dated 1890. *Innsbruck, Tiroler Landesmuseum Ferdinandeum.*

409 Art Nouveau frame on the same board as the painting "Lady with Mask" by Hans Pellar (1886-1971), dated 1909. *Cologne, von Abecron.*

410   Art Nouveau frame on the same board as the painting "Christmas" by Hans Pellar, dated 1910. *Cologne, von Abecron.*

411   Frame as integral part of the painting "Song of Eternity" by Jan Toorp (1858-1928), dated 1893. *Otterlo, Museum Kröller-Müller.*

412   Art Nouveau frame made for "Masked Ball" by Hans Pellar, c.1907. *Cologne, von Abecron.*

413   Plate frame with inlaid tablets bearing inscriptions in Arabic, made for the portrait of Clemens Pausinger (1855-1936), dated 1929. *London, Galleria dell'Angelo.*

414   Art Nouveau frame with extra large *kymation* on the inner border and an undulating band on the plate. Made for a portrait of Franz von Stuck (1863-1928), c.1900. *Cologne, von Abecron.*

415   Art Nouveau frame with enlarged *kymation* and volute ornaments, silver-plated. Made for a portrait of Franz von Stuck, dated 1911. *Cologne, von Abecron.*

416   Art Nouveau frame with a surface made from modelling clay. Not made for the picture it now houses. c.1905. *Cologne, von Abecron.*

417 Impressionist frame, consisting of an antiquarian frame, preferably in Louis XIV style, thinly covered with bright paint. The mixture of new color and the old gilt results in the desired effect. The example illustrated belongs to "Soleil couchant à Eragny" by Camille Pissarro (1831-1903), dated 1902. From the Pissarro estate. *Oxford, Ashmolean Museum.*

418 Pointillist frame with dotted plate and narrow outer border. Made for "The Garden at Calmpthout" by Henry van de Velde (1863-1957), c.1890. *Munich, Bayerische Staatsgemäldesammlungen.*

419   Detail from illus. 418.

Folk Art

420 Spanish plate frame with multi-colored painted ornamentation, interrupted by marbelized sections. 17th century. *Berlin, Lemke.*

421 Spanish plate frame with green flowers and blossoms, heightened with gold. Andalusia, early 18th century. *Berlin, Lemke.*

422 Spanish plate frame with multi-colored ornamentation. Early 18th century. *Berlin, Lemke.*

Folk Art

423 Stylistic anachronism in folk art: multi-colored frame in Louis XVI style for a devotional image. Upper Bavaria, between 1810 and 1820. *Munich, Bayerisches Nationalmuseum.*

424 Frame with ornamentation in the manner of the Louis XVI style with an infusion of older popular baroque patterns (fish-scale and parallelograms, and volutes), in red and gold. Upper Bavaria, between 1810 and 1820. *Nuremberg, Germanisches Nationalmuseum.*

425 Frame surmounted by a segment painted in multi-color and rococo Louis XV corner ornaments. Stylistically contemporary with the backs of the beds in the devotional image it houses. Bavarian, dated 1792. *Munich, Bayerisches Nationalmuseum.*

426 Frame structure with satin and mirrors for a "Flagellation of Christ." School of Ayacucho, Peru; 17/18th century. *Rome, Private Collection.*

Folk Art

427 Mannerist frame for a Madonna by Bernardo Bilti (1548-1610). Probably from Cuzco, Peru; early 17th century. *La Paz, Private Collection.*

428 Wooden frame with superimposed embossings for the pilgrimage church "Mother of God, Help Us Poor Souls." Decorated with silver foil ornaments and wide center and corner cartouches, dated 1681. *Pilgrimage Church, Mariahilf,*

429   Mexican luxury frame with coral in white, blue, red and gold. 17th century. *Paris, Lebrun.*

Small Formats

430 Carved leaf and blossom frame (height 17 cm). Presumably made for a devotional image or object. Wood. Alpine, 17th century. *Munich, Riggauer.*

431 Leaf frame with single convex profile. Alpine or southern German, late 18th century. Munich, 18th century.

432 Small frame with shallow channel, black base, and painted gold ornamentation. South German, 18th century.

433 Popular small oval frame; black base with colored floral ornaments. Franconia or Tyrol, 18th century. *Munich, Riggauer.*

434 Leaf frame, southern German or Austrian, reflecting Italian influence; 18th century. *Munich, Riggauer.*

435   Small plate frame, gilded. South German or Austrian, late 18th century. *Munich, Riggauer.*

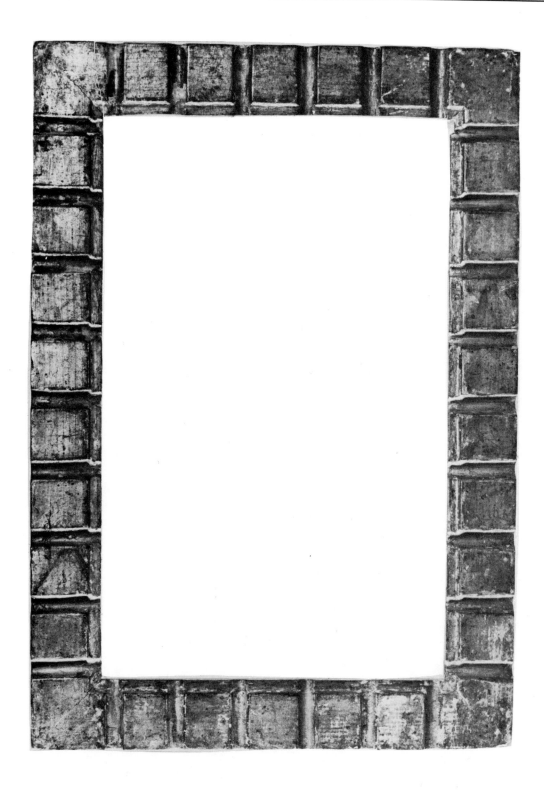

436   Small model frame made from a single piece of wood. South German, c.1765. *Munich, Riggauer.*

437 Frame as woodcarver's experiment. Made of oak in the shape of a ruined portal with ivy vines. South German (?);
late 18th century. *Munich, Riggauer.*

438 Choice of frame based on considerations of color or structural elements of the picture it houses: mirror frame with ornamentation made in the 19th century, used for a still life with silver vase by Pieter Roestraten (1630-1700). *Amsterdam, Rijksmuseum.*

Variations of Present-Day Museum Frames

439 Early 16th century Florentine mirror frame (lacking the superstructure), housing a portrait by Jacometto Veneziano, painted between 1472 and 1497. *London, National Gallery.*

440 New, wide frame, made of natural wood, surrounding, for the purpose of optical strengthening, the original (!), visible black frame of the portrait of Hieronymus Holzschuher by Albrecht Dürer (1471-1528), painted in 1526. *Berlin-Dahlem, Gamäldegalerie.*

441   New frame, made c.1903, for the altarpiece by Carlo Crivelli, dated 1486. The decorative frame dupicates the ornamentation of the painted pillar. *London, National Gallery.*

Variations of Present-Day Museum Frames

442 Example of classical leaf, blossom, and fruit carvings in a modern frame. *Copenhagen, Statens Museeum for Kunst.*

443 Example of the use of decorative details of a painting in narrow, newly added frames. *Rotterdam, Museum Boymans-van Beuningen.*

444 Example of the refusal to use non-authentic frames: "The Erbach Tablet," having "The Apocalypse" as its subject. Neapolitan, c.1340, displayed in a plexiglass case. *Stuttgart, Staatsgalerie.*

445 Example of the use of expressive rustic forms: relief by Paul Gauguin (1848-1903) in a coarse variant of an Italian ornamental leaf frame of the 17th century. *Copenhagen, Ny Carlsberg Glyptithel.*

Variations of Present-Day Museum Frames

446 Use of popular baroque edges and ornaments as superimposed decoration of a plate frame. The arrangement follows late Gothic and popular early baroque models, although in an uncustomary juxtaposition of the ornaments and the metallic base. The frame is a subsequent addition for the painting "The Offer of Sacrifice" by Georges Lacombe (1868-1916). *Bremen, Kunsthalle.*

447 Example of the use of a recently acquired historical frame that corresponds in function and style to the picture it houses: "Portrait of a Standing Officer," presumed to represent captain of infantry Alessandro del Borro, painted by an anonymous Tuscan painter, c.1645. The frame is a large plate type with the three-bee emblem of the Barberini family used in the ornamentation, as well as the Barberini escutcheons in the centers of the lateral members with a cardinal's hat. It can therefore be related to Pope Urban VIII, Maffeo Barberini, when he was still a cardinal, **i.e.** before 1623, or subsequently his nephews, Francesco or Antonio Barberini. Capt. Borro had dealings with the Barberini's in the capacity of an enemy. *Berlin-Dahlem, Gemäldegalerie.*

Frames for Graphics

448-50 Corners of mahogany frames which house passe-partouts behind glass. The simple ones are made from smooth, reddish-brown wood with, sometimes raised, black or brown corners. The more elaborate examples are decorated with inlaid wood or brass rosettes. Neoclassical, early 19th century. *Munich, Riggauer.*

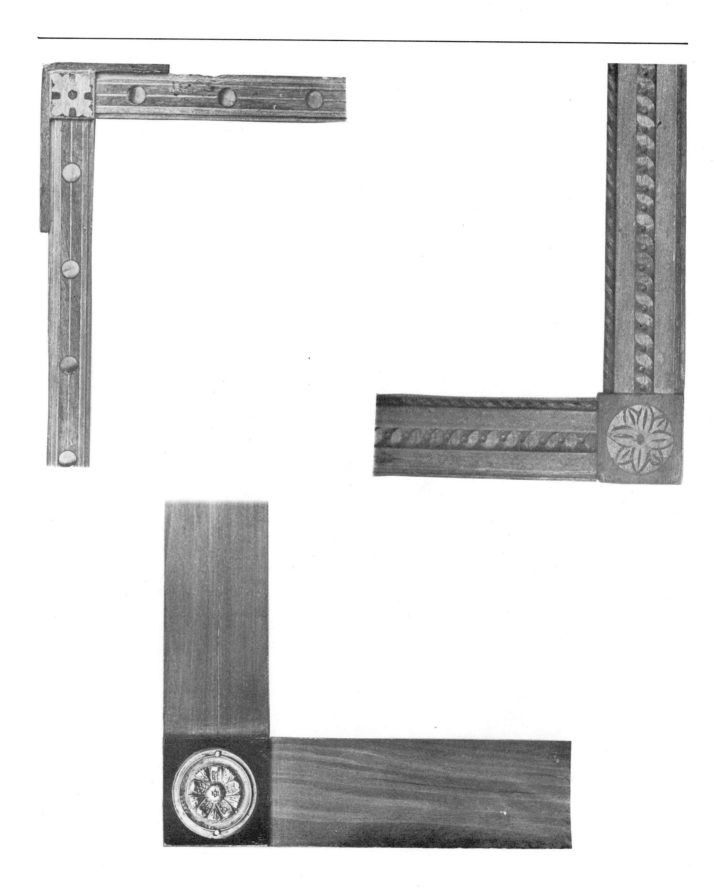

451-452   Louis XVI frame and other neoclassical, narrow molding frames, gilded or silvered, used for passe-partouts. Late 18th century. *Private Collection.*

Frames for Graphics

453 Example of a small carved frame for which it is usually difficult to find an aesthetically suitable painting, without diminishing the effect. Attempts to use such frames for prints or drawings visually fail. Carved and gilded frame. Mid-18th century. *Munich, Riggauer.*

Frames in America

A pioneering work like this one by Claus Grimm on the history of European picture frames needs no elucidation. His commentary is comprehensive and succinct, and serves as a guide to the function, development, art and esthetic of frames. The rich illustrative material constitutes the first pictorial survey of this uniquely Western art form.

This translation widens the audience to include English-speaking readers, and this occasion coupled with the fact that it is published here, in the United States, are perhaps my only excuses for adding a chapter on American frames to this ground-breaking and indispensable handbook.

A third, purely personal reason has persuaded me to prepare this supplementary section: For the past two decades a unique collection of antique frames of all periods in the Robert Lehman collection, now in the Metropolitan Museum of Art, has been in my charge. In the course of conserving, cataloguing, and occasionally exhibiting these frames, I have been confronted with the very problems which are discussed in this volume. I have also frequently had to face the dilemma of how and when to use some of these historical frames for exhibiting drawings. As a consequence, some thoughts and conclusions about the history of framing and matting drawings are offered in the following pages, even though briefly.

The English word "frame" has a variety of origins, and is endowed with a number of meanings. Interestingly enough, these meanings all apply, and have reference to the making, function, art and esthetic of the picture frame, and relate importantly to the principal points made in this book. The word "frame," as it is used today, derives from the Middle English "framen" meaning "structure." In turn, this probably has two roots: the Old English "framian," i.e., "to be helpful," and the Old Nordic "frami," i.e., "profit" or "benefit." In early English usage, like today, "to frame" also means "to shape," "to construct," "to enclose within a border," and finally, "to adapt for a particular use."

This synopsis of the etymology and usage of the word contains within its "framework" the basic outline for a historical evaluation of picture frames. The frame is a structure created especially for the benefit of a picture, in order to protect it. The materials utilized for the construction of a frame are adapted for this particular use, that is, they are joined, shaped, and decorated by using various techniques. Its ornamentation—whether purely decorative or augmented by components such as a date, coat of arms, emblems or inscriptions—serves to enhance the function, meaning and value of the picture. To frame, that is "to enclose within a border," is an esthetic function: in this quality it defines the pictorial space, sets and regulates it. Moreover it offers an opportunity for the artist's imagination in other modes of expression: to plan, devise, contrive, or compose; to invent or fabricate, to express or utter, to conceive or imagine anything that is "framed in his mind."

There are no known or surviving picture frames from the early cultures and arts of the Americas. However, there are traces of definition of pictorial and relief spaces and fields by the use of framework, composed of ornamental elements or pictographs on many carved stone stelae (e.g. Piedras Negras; cf. P. Kelemen, *Medieval American Art,* New York

1956, pls. 72, 77). Therefore a similarity to the European concept of defining pictorial space by means of framing is evident, despite the predominantly Asiatic affinities of the arts in Early America. Mirror frames for obsidian and other polished stone mirrors, carved of wood and gilded or painted, are closer to the European concept of frames; some are decorated as elaborately as their 13th-14th century Western European counterparts (cf. Kelemen, *op. cit.* pl. 298).

The earliest European frames must have arrived in America with the conquistadores for the protection of sacred pictures. Inventories of Spanish and Portuguese ships list small devotional pictures aboard naval as well as commercial vessels. Their style and framing presumably were of the then-current 16th and 17th century types prevailing in those countries. These pictures and their frames were probably imitated immediately for the furnishings of newly erected churches, chapels, and monastic buildings. Their somewhat simplified, yet still sumptuous decoration is well demonstrated in surviving examples (nos. 148, 149).

The wealth of early colonial mining towns and the availability of precious metals contributed to the creation of innovative gold and silver frames. Although they imitate the European manner and decorative patterns, these somewhat crude, locally designed and produced works are probably the first indigenous American frames (Artemio De Valle Arizpe, *Notas de plateria,* Mexico City 1961, *passim*).

In the north, English and Dutch settlers brought along different types of pictures and frames. Religious beliefs and rules prohibited graven or painted holy images. However, portraits of sovereigns and likenesses of family members must have been part of the furnishings of the early settlements. These pictures were probably transported and kept in frames. Although there is no clearly identifiable 17th century Dutch picture frame in the American colonies, we can resort to analogies from other Dutch colonies. For example, in 1669, Pieter de Wit painted a full-length portrait of the Dutch merchant Dirck Wilre, standing in his room in Elmina Castle on Africa's Gold Coast. The walls of the chamber are lined with gilt-leather wall covering, probably made in Antwerp. In the center a black slave displays a Dutch landscape painting in an elaborate frame similar to the so-called "Lutma" frames of the mid-17th century (cf. W.H. Vroom, "Dirck Wilre in Elmina" *Bulletin van het Rijksmuseum,* vol. 27, 1979, p. 8).

In the cities of colonial America framemaking was part of the trade of the looking-glass and cabinet makers. In Philadelphia, two generations of Elliots, John Sr. and John Jr., maintained a shop in which they sold, made and repaired looking glasses and frames "plain, gilt and carved and of mahogany" between 1756 and 1809 (cf. A.C. Prime, "John Elliot, Cabinet and Looking Glass Maker in Philadelphia," *The Pennsylvania Museum Bulletin,* vol. 19, 1924, pp. 127-39). From contemporary advertisements it is evident that several craftsmen offered their wares and services: *The Federal Gazette* on April 23, 1791 informs that "John McElwee has for sale a quantity of gilt and black and gilt carved mouldings of different sizes for looking glasses and picture frames. Orders from any part of the continent executed with punctuality and dispatch." These common sources for frames from Philadelphia, Boston, and Baltimore account primarily for the relative uniformity of frames on early American paintings. This pattern is broken only when either the owners designed and made their own picture frames, or artists provided specially designed and carved framing for their paintings.

Charles Wilson Peale frequently noted sizes or specifications for the frames he intended for his canvases. These were usually provided by his brother James Peale, who had been trained by him as a framer and gilder. He also commissioned frames, such as in 1791 from James Reynolds, a Philadelphia carver and gilder (cf. C.C. Sellers, "Portraits and Miniatures by Charles Wilson Peale," *Transactions of the American Philosophical Society,* Philadelphia 1953, vol. 42, p. 19).

Many late 18th century American portraits still retain their original carved and gilt—and sometimes very elaborate—frames. Yet there are also a considerable number of original frames which are quite simple: made of run-of-the-mill molding that was sold by the foot and ornamented with painted or stencilled decorations simulating marble or ivory, and often embellished with inscriptions. These painted frames are the earliest examples of the trompe l'oeil decoration that became so fashionable during the middle of the century. This American fascination with deceiving the eye and playing with the limitation of the pictorial field by—or its extension into—the frame, or the intrusion of the framework into the painting itself continued through the 19th century and is still very much alive (N.F. Little, "Picture Frames with Painted Decoration 1775-1850," *Antiques,* September 1958, pp. 242-45; and

M.L. d'Otrange Mastai, *Illusion in Art. Trompe l'Oeil, A History of Pictorial Illusion.* New York, Abaris Books 1975, pp. 259-317).

Mid-century family portraits and views of interiors provide a fascinating record of how pictures were used and hung in American homes, especially in New England. Both ornate and simpler frames were suspended from nails, brass pins or rods by means of cords and ribbons. Treatises on homemaking and furnishings devoted remarks to proper framing and hanging: "In hanging up pictures around a room, they should be placed so that the lower parts are not above the eye of an observer. It prevents defacing the wall, if there are many pictures, to have long brass rods at the top of the wall from which the pictures can be suspended, by cords or ribands, which should all be of color." (B.T. Rumford, "How Pictures Were Used in New England Houses, 1825-1850," *Antiques,* November 1974, pp. 827-55.)

In the second half of the 19th century, the destruction of the Civil War, the accumulation of wealth in the North and East, and the great westward expansion of the country created an enormous need for home furnishings and likewise for frames. Almost every European style was widely imitated in frames manufactured by advanced methods, using carving machinery, plate casting, and inexpensive gilding. The mass-produced frames were advertised in catalogues and marketed by the pioneers of the mail order business, thereby spreading an almost uniform style from Maine to the Carolinas, from the big Eastern industrial cities to the rich little mining towns in Colorado.

The creation of individual frames, however, still flourished in the art centers. The romantic frames of France and England have their counterparts in America. The carefully planned frames by the great artists of the late 19th century influenced many in America (cf. A. Grieve, "The Applied Art of D.G. Rossetti.I. His Picture Frames," *The Burlington Magazine,* vol. 115, 1973, pp. 16-23; I.M. Horowitz, "Whistler's Frames," *Art Journal,* vol. 39, 1979/80, pp. 124-31). The eclectic taste at the end of the century produced elaborate frameworks designed and inspired by the tastemakers in architecture and interior decoration, among them Stanford White and Louis Comfort Tiffany. Elaborate carvings, exquisitely painted moldings, inlays of gold-glass and gesso reliefs abound on these frames, which were produced primarily on commission; sometimes in pairs for matching paintings.

The most original and enchanting frames were crafted after the turn of the century by Charles Prendergast of Boston. The noble dedication of the Pre-Raphaelites, the old American tradition of whittling, and the profound interest in the decorative arts of the Renaissance permeates his carved and gessoed frames. The incised and punched floral motifs, closely following those of the Sienese and Florentine primitives, and the subtle use of color distinguish these artistic creations. They are in perfect harmony with his own paintings and with those of his brother, Maurice Prendergast. These frames not only enhance the pictures, but sometimes assume a significance far beyond their so-called functional or secondary role; they are works of art on their own merit (R.J. Wattenmaker, *The Art of Charles Prendergast,* Rutgers University, Museum of Fine Arts, Boston 1968).

This devotion to the art and craft of framemaking by Prendergast and other American artists was greatly nurtured by the presence of outstanding frames in American museums and private collections. Fenway Court, the Museum of Fine Arts, the Wadsworth Athenaeum, the Jarvis Collection at Yale University, and the Metropolitan Museum of Art must have given considerable impetus and inspiration to the development of this art form in the Western hemisphere. The great collectors at the turn of the century brought to American cities an immense number of old and contemporary frames, thereby fully integrating their own development with that in various European art centers.

Today these same institutions and some new ones are striving not only to embellish and enhance their pictures with proper historical frames, but also to maintain collections of frames. The National Gallery of Art with the help of the Kress Foundation, the Metropolitan Museum of Art, and even private collectors are preserving, cataloguing and exhibiting frames, not only on pictures but also as autonomous works of art (G. Szabo, *Renaissance Decorative Arts from the Robert Lehmann Collection of the Metropolitan Museum of Art,* Tokyo 1977, nos. 86-95). Notable is the fact, however, that no exhibition in America has as yet been fully devoted to the art and history of picture frames.

Frames for Drawings

The use of old frames in today's museums poses a number of problems. Conservation is one of them: many old frames have to be completely restored and their structure strengthened to support panel paintings and even canvases. However, the main task is to have the old frame conform to a picture both physically and esthetically. To solve the first often requires changing or altering the dimensions of the frame; this is impossible in most cases since such alterations would damage a work of art. A more practical solution is the utilization of various inner frames and mattings to harmonize with the proportions of the picture and the framework. The aesthetic "fitting" is seemingly a matter of individual taste; it is successful in the case of portraits or small religious subjects or when Impressionist paintings are placed in 18th century French frames.

The most promising and successful use of old frames, however, seems to have been found in the exhibition of old master drawings. Most frequently, drawings are shown in so-called uniform frames, usually made of simple strip-molds either stained or gilt. Although it has been asserted that these simple frames interfere only minimally with the drawings exhibited in them, they tend to give an appearance of monotony to an exhibition hall. Their use has also been defended by reference to the century-old practice of keeping and preserving drawings in portfolios or most recently, matted and stored in boxes. It has also often been claimed that drawings were never kept or exhibited in frames.

It is true that the earliest known compilations of drawings—we may call them collections—are in bound volumes or affixed to especially decorated sheets of paper. Of this, the so-called "Sketchbook of Jacopo Bellini" or "Il Libro dei Disegni" of Giorgio Vasari are the best known examples. However, as early as the first decade of the 16th century, drawings were kept and probably displayed in frames. Albrecht Dürer during his trip to the Netherlands in 1520-1521, recorded among his expenses payments for frames of drawings. He carefully notes, "I drew portraits of Bernard Stecher and his wife . . . and I made another portrait of his wife and had a frame made for it for 6 st." Even more interesting is another of Dürer's notations in which he describes a frame of a different type: "I drew Master Jacob's portrait in charcoal and had a tablet frame made more elaborate. Most likely it had a backing for it—cost 6 st." While the first frame probably was a simple structure, the second was made of wood or some kind of sliding cover to protect the front of the image. In this respect Dürer's tablet-frame resembles the one represented on the early 17th century Flemish gallery painting "Cognoscenti in a Room Hung with Pictures" in the National Gallery, London (Fig. 482). The figure on the left holds this frame displaying a drawing with insects and snails in the manner of Hoefnagel, with its protective cover pulled out.

This frame and others are very similar to those usually referred to as "Nun's Mirrors" which most likely served the same purpose as the one depicted on the painting.

A number of 17th century Dutch and Flemish frames were probably made for the display of drawings, particularly for larger and treasured ones; old mattings and notations on some bear testimony to this. A century later in France not only frames but also elaborate mats were designed and decorated for the exclusive purpose of displaying drawings. Especially in Paris, several artist-draftsmen specialized in this trade. The best known among them was probably Jean-Baptiste Glomy, who during the reign of Louis XV maintained a shop at the corner of rue Bourbon and rue Saint-Claude. Although no signed or marked frame by him exists today, a rare marbelized mat, stamped with his dry-stamp "GLOMY" is found on a drawing in the Robert Lehman Collection, Metropolitan Museum of Art. He died in 1786, but his name is still recalled by the term "églomisé," a technique of ancient origin using gold and painted glass panels which Glomy frequently employed on his frames. (P.G. "Toute la verité sur le verre 'églomisé.'" *Connaissance des Arts,* no. 66. 1957. pp. 28-33.)

Most old frames, even those from periods when frames were already used for drawings, are too heavy and overpowering for them. However, certain types seem to be easily adaptable and greatly enhance drawings which are exhibited in them. Some 17th century Northern frames (nos. 162-164, 171, 176) are compatible not only with contemporary Dutch or Flemish drawings but also with earlier ones from Northern Europe.

Inlaid ebony frames or those covered with tortoise shell, frame Northern drawings superbly, and enhance their preciousness and rarity. Similarly many 18th century Italian, especially Venetian frames, are well suited to exhibit drawings. Whether they are plain or decorated with paint, lacquer or gilt (cf. nos. 220-222) or more elaborately carved, these frames compliment and flatter the drawings they enclose.

The frames of the various revival styles of the 19th century are used quite frequently as well as are those made especially for the famous collectors of the late 19th and early 20th centuries. Today exact copies and imitations of important old frames are frequently made and sometimes even mass produced to satisfy the demand for so-called "proper period frames." Fortunately, a few distinguished collectors still attempt to collect and preserve old frames and whenever possible, use them to enhance their drawings and paintings.

Bibliography

Covi, Dario. A XIV century Italian Altarpiece, *The Bulletin of the Metropolitan Museum of Art,* vol. 16. 1958. pp. 147-55.

Eisler, Colin. Verre églomisé and Paolo di Giovanni Fei, *Journal of Glass Studies,* vol. 3. 1961. pp. 30-36.

Heckscher, Morrison H. Gideon Saint, An Eighteenth Century Carver and His Scrapbook, *The Bulletin of the Metropolitan Museum of Art,* vol. 27. 1969. pp. 299-311.

Szabo, George. *XV century Italian Drawings from the Robert Lehman Collection, New York,* The Metropolitan Museum of Art, 1978. no. 11.

Szabo, George. *XVII century Dutch and Flemish Drawings from the Robert Lehman Collection, New York,* The Metropolitan Museum of Art, 1979, no. 52b.

454-55 *Portraits of Mr. and Mrs. Joseph Reade,* by John Wollaston (American, active 1736-1767). The portraits are in their original carved and gilded frames, probably produced by a local American framemaker. *New York, The Metropolitan Museum of Art.*

456 *Portrait of Samuel Verplanck* (1739-1820), by John Singleton Copley (American, 1738-1815). The portrait was painted in New York in 1771; the modified and simplified George III frame is probably a local product. *New York, The Metropolitan Museum of Art, Gift of James Delancey Verplanck, 1939.*

457 *Portrait of Mrs. Jerathmael Bowers,* by John Singleton Copley (American, 1738-1815). Both the portrait and the original frame are clearly influenced by the most fashionable English types of the time. *New York, The Metropolitan Museum of Art.*

458 *The Falls of Niagara,* by Edward Hicks (American, 1780-1849). The title and the date, 1825, are painted in the four corners. The sides are further embellished by four two-line quotations from Alexander Wilson's "The Forester" written 1809-1810. *New York, The Metropolitan Museum of Art.*

459 *Roses by Trunk of a Tree,* by John O'Brien (1828-1896). Signed and dated 1869 in the original frame designed by the artist. *New York, The Kennedy Galleries.*

460-61 *Still Life with Roses* (Pair), by George C. Lambdin (1830-1896). Signed and dated 1878, the pair of panels is in the original matching frames designed by the artist with somber Neo-Classical elements. *New York, The Collection of Mrs. Charles Goldman.*

462 *Tobit and the Angel,* by Thomas Dewing (American, 1851-1938). The painting is dated 1887 and its original
frame was probably designed by Stanford White. *New York, The Metropolitan Museum of Art.*

463 *Alexander Stewart Wetherill,* by Alfred Q. Collins (American). The young boy was Stanford White's nephew and it is known that the famous architect commissioned the painting and designed the frame in the 1890's. *New York, The Metropolitan Museum of Art.*

464 *Portrait of Augustus Saint-Gaudens,* by Kenyon Cox (American, 1856-1919). Replica of a lost portrait repainted by the artist with the understanding that it would be presented to the Metropolitan Museum of Art on the occasion of the Saint-Gaudens memorial exhibition in 1908. The frame with the laurel wreaths was also designed by Cox. *New York, The Metropolitan Museum of Art.*

465 Frame, carved, gilded and silvered wood, decorated with incised floral design in corners. Charles Prendergast (American, 1863-1948). *New York, The Metropolitan Museum of Art, The Robert Lehman Collection, 1975.*

466 *Portrait of Ralph Dusenberry,* by Arthur G. Dove (1880-1946). *New York, The Metropolitan Museum of Art, The Alfred Stieglitz Collection, 1949.*

467 *The Visit of Ulysses S. Grant to India,* by Erastus Salisbury Field (1805-1900). Oil on canvas with illusionistic frame. *Museum of Fine Arts, Springfield (Mass.), The Morgan Wesson Memorial Collection.*

468 *An Egyptian Sarcophagus,* by Erastus Salisbury Field (1805-1900). Oil on canvas with illusionistic frame. *Museum of Fine Arts, Springfield (Mass.), The Morgan Wesson Memorial Collection.*

469 Design for an altarpiece of the "Madonna della Misercordia." Venetian artist, circa 1400. An early design for an elaborate painted and carved framework similar in manner to that on the Brunelleschi altarpiece (no. 470). *New York, The Metropolitan Museum of Art, The Robert Lehman Collection, 1975.*

470 *Altarpiece with the Coronation of the Virgin, with Saints Bernard, Sylvester, Nicholas and Julian.* Italian artist, Florence, 1394. The large altarpiece is decorated with the portraits of the donors, with their coat-of-arms and a dedicatory inscription that reads: "HANC TABVLAM FIERI ALDEROTVS DE BRVNELLESCHIS QVE DIMISSIT SILVESTER PATRVVS SVVS PRO REMEDIO ANIME SVE E SVORUM A D M CCC L XXXX IIII" and continues "DIE VIIII MENSIS NOVENBRIS." *New York, The Metropolitan Museum of Art, Gift of Robert Lehman, 1950.*

471 Detail from no. 472. Lower left corner of frame with the details of the punched-in decoration and verre églomisé medallion with St. John the Evangelist.

472   *Madonna and Child,* by Paolo di Giovanni Fei (Sienese, circa 1342-1410). Frame with gessoed, punched-in decoration embellished with glass-paste beads and verre-églomisé roundels representing the Virgin of Annunciation, the Archangel Gabriel and various saints. *New York, The Metropolitan Museum of Art, Bequest of George Blumenthal, 1941.*

473 *Virgin and Child.* French artist, probably Burgundian, early XV century. Frame carved of the same wood as the panel; "comprehensible traditional decorative elements are combined with a transitional form toward the molded frame." *New York, The Frick Collection.*

474 *Madonna and Child in Landscape,* by Jan Gossaert de Mabuse (circa 1478-1532). Signed and dated 1531. The original frame also painted by the artist is inscribed in two "tabula ansata": TVA MATER CONTEMPLATIO NOSTRI SIT RECONCILIATIO. *Cleveland, Ohio, The Cleveland Museum of Art, Purchase John L. Severance Fund.*

475 Detail from lower right corner of no. 474.

476 Design for a picture frame by Antoine Waterloo (Dutch, 1610-1690). The design and its details are very similar to those on the so-called Lutma frames such as nos. 180-181. The artist's wife, Catharyn Stevens van den Dorpe was a dealer in pictures and it is possible that the design was done in connection with her business. *New York, The Metropolitan Museum of Art, The Robert Lehman Collection, 1975.*

477 Scrapbook compiled about 1763-1768, by Gideon Saint (British, 1729-1799). Working drawing for the ornamentation of a picture frame, found in the scrapbook. The paper with the brown ink design was folded and then pricked to obtain a symmetrical image. It was transferred to the frame probably with the use of charcoal powder or powdered paint. *New York, The Metropolitan Museum of Art, Harris Brisbane Dick Fund, 1934.*

478 Scrapbook compiled about 1763-1768, by Gideon Saint (British, 1729-1799). Designs and patterns for picture frames, some engraved, most in ink and wash, numbered and annotated by Saint whose shop was on Princes Street in London. *New York, The Metropolitan Museum of Art, Harris Brisbane Dick Fund, 1934.*

Frames in America

479 Scrapbook compiled about 1763-1799, by Gideon Saint (British, 172901799). Patterns and cross-sections of frame mouldings; these working drawings clearly demonstrate the variety of motifs and the careful annotations such as "sanded," etc. give details of the methods used. *New York, The Metropolitan Museum of Art, Harris Brisbane Dick Fund, 1934.*

480 So-called "Nun's Mirror," possibly covered frame for drawings. Italian, early XVII century. This frame with sliding cover. It is comparable to that represented on the early XVII century painting of "Cognoscenti" in the National Gallery in London. *The Metropolitan Museum of Art, The Robert Lehman Collection, 1975.*

481 "Nun's Mirror" with open cover.

Frames for Drawings

482   *Cognoscenti in a Room Hung with Pictures.* Flemish painter, circa 1620. A great variety of frames is represented on this typical early XVII century Flemish gallery painting. They range from the simple moulds to the profusely decorated, and display a wide variety of embellishments such as stencil painting, metal mounts and gilt carving. *London, The National Gallery.*

483   *Cognoscenti in a Room Hung with Pictures* (detail). Flemish painter, circa 1620. Frame for drawing with retractable cover displayed by the person on the left, while the one on the right holds a small framed drawing. Unframed sheets are strewn around and a large folio displays various prints by Dürer and Lucas van Leyden. *London, The National Gallery.*

Frames for Drawings

484 Composite frame for individually framed smaller drawings attributed to Albrecht Dürer. Mid-XVI century, Spanish (70 x 60 cm). Formerly in the antechamber of Philip II's bedroom in the Escorial Palace. No longer extant. *Photo Courtesy R.K.D., The Hague.*

485   Frame, Dutch, XVII century. The profiled wood-moulding is completely covered with pressed tortoise-shell that is glued to the core and then polished and varnished. The natural pattern and warm tones are especially favorable for XVI-XVII century Northern drawings. *New York, The Metropolitan Museum of Art, The Robert Lehman Collection, 1975.*

Frames for Drawings

486   Frame, Italian, possibly Venetian, XVIII century. Carved wood covered with gesso and gilt possibly with the original forged iron hook. *New York, The Metropolitan Museum of Art, The Robert Lehman Collection, 1975.*

487 *Equestrian Statue of Hadrian,* by Hubert Robert (1733-1808). The drawing, which may be dated circa 1757, is in its original mat that bears the dry-stamp "Glomy." It is probably the work of Jean-Baptiste Glomy, the XVIII century French artist/frame-maker (died in 1786). His frames were decorated with glass panels, painted and gilt on the back, the technique he revitalized and which is now named, after him, "églomisé." *New York, The Metropolitan Museum of Art, The Robert Lehman Collection, 1975.*

488   Frame, carved and inlaid. Attributed to Gerard van Opstal (1605-1668). The exquisitely designed and carved
      wood frame is decorated with putti bearing the symbols of the cardinal virtues. It was most likely created for
      a portrait and attributed to the Brussels artist Gerard van Opstal. *Collection of Mr. Paul Doll, Berkeley Heights,*
      N.J.

489 Detail of no. 488.